# Rebuild

## A Family's Journey
## the First Year
## After a Stroke

*To: Norm*

*You have been someone I have always looked up to. I miss our conversations where we solve all of the worlds problems :)*

*Join us on the journey in the pages of this book.*

*LAUGH, CRY & REJOICE with US.*

*MAY 10 2022*

By

**Andrew Smith**

Kipekee Press

Rebuilding Janise:
A Family's Journey in the First Year After a Stroke

Copyright © 2022 by Andrew Smith

Hardcover ISBN: 978-1-9992982-7-2
Paperback ISBN: 978-1-9992982-5-8
e-book ISBN: 978-1-9992982-6-5
Audiobook: 978-1-9992982

A percentage of the net proceeds of sales of this book will go to Heart & Stroke Foundation Canada charity to support families affected by strokes.

Kipekee Press
600 Rossland Road, Oshawa, ON, Canada L1J 8M7
www.kipekeepress.com

# DEDICATION

To my best friend, teenage love, girlfriend, lover, wife, baby mama, ride or die, biggest fan, cheerleader, life partner and soul mate: Janise Anne Marie Smith ♥. It has been amazing sharing the journey we call life together with you on this planet.

To our legacy: our boys Jabari Adio Smith and Jelani Akil Smith, the manifestation of the verb we cherish most LOVE♥. You continue to exceed all expectations, all boxes, all limitations. The court-side seats to your journey, your life, are in a word, priceless!

# CONTENTS

**POEM: I AM**

**INTRODUCTION**

**PART 1: ALL HELL BREAKS LOOSE**

March 18th – When Things Fell Apart ........................................................ 14

March 20th – What the HELL is a THALAMUS ........................................ 16

March 28th – "Until the end of time" ........................................................ 18

March 29th – Pain ........................................................................................ 19

March 30th – "Can you stand the rain" .................................................... 20

March 31st – The Past, The Present ......................................................... 22

April 1st – Competition .............................................................................. 24

April 2nd – Dynamic Light ......................................................................... 26

April 3rd – The Brain .................................................................................. 27

April 4th – Great Lessons .......................................................................... 28

April 5th – Medicine of the Past ............................................................... 30

April 6th – Everything will work out ......................................................... 31

April 6th – Andrew ...................................................................................... 32

April 7th – Thankful .................................................................................... 33

April 8th – "Ribbon in the Sky" ................................................................ 35

April 9th – "Stand" ...................................................................................... 36

April 10th – Walking .................................................................................... 38

**PART II: REHABILITATION**

April 11th – Unplugged .............................................................................. 42

April 12th – Purpose ................................................................................... 43

April 13th – New Spaces ............................................................................ 45

April 13th – Familiar Truths ...................................................................... 46

April 15th – The Law of Inertia ................................................................. 47

April 16th – Man Plans and God Laughs ................................................. 49

April 17th – Happy Endings ....................................................................... 51

April 18th – Pop Quiz ................................................................................. 53

April 19th – Dance ...................................................................................... 54

April 20th – Good Friday ............................................................................ 55

April 21st – Afro .......................................................................................... 57

April 21st – "Chant a Psalms a Day" ....................................................... 59

April 23rd – Women and Their Relationships .......................................... 61

April 24th – Moving to Providence ............... 63

April 24th - "Get Here" ............... 64

April 26th - The List ............... 66

April 27th - "Alright" ............... 68

April 28th - Change ............... 69

April 30th - The Providence Routine ............... 70

May 1st – Talk 2 Me ............... 72

May 2nd – Cold Shower ............... 74

May 3rd – "Everybody's Got a Thing" ............... 76

May 5th – Prevention & Rehabilitation ............... 78

May 5th – "I'm Ready" ............... 80

May 7th – "Free" ............... 82

May 7th – OK ............... 83

May 8th – Baseball Practice ............... 85

May 10th – "Feels Good" ............... 86

May 10th – Communication ............... 88

May 11th – Task List ............... 90

May 12th – Mothers' Day ............... 92

May 13th – "All Day All Night" ............... 93

May 14th – Appointments ............... 94

May 15th – Time ............... 96

May 16th – Fuel for the Tank ............... 97

May 19th – Game Day ............... 99

May 20th – The Long Weekend ............... 101

May 22nd – Back 2 the Future ............... 103

May 23rd – Home 4 the Weekend ............... 105

May 25th – Shamiso's Wedding ............... 107

May 25th – Advice for the Young Couple ............... 110

May 27th – Living 4 the Weekend ............... 111

May 28th – "Count the Days" ............... 112

May 29th – Needs & Wants ............... 113

May 30th – "Home" ............... 115

**PART III: HOME AT LAST!**

June 1st – Man's World? ............... 118

June 2nd – Mighty & Brave ............... 120

June 4th – Familiarity ............... 122

June 4th – "I'd Rather Be with You" — 123
June 6th – Spring — 125
June 6th – Memories — 127
June 9th –"...& God Created Woman" — 128
June 12th – Advocacy — 130
June 12th – Irie — 131
June 15th – "Unconditional" — 133
June 16th – Kitchener — 135
June 18th –"We Are One" — 137
June 19th – Just the Facts — 139
June 20th – Questions — 141
June 23rd – Road Trip — 143
June 25th – Helping vs. Independence — 145
June 26th – The View U Have of U — 147
June 26th – "Joy in Repetition" — 149

July 1st – It's the Weekend Baby! — 151
July 3rd – Who Are You? — 153

**PART IV: NEW NORMAL**
July 5th – Going Down — 158
July 7th – Your Garden — 160
July 9th – Our Brain — 162
July 11th – Golden Shower — 164
July 12th – Speechless — 166
July 15th – Toronto Beach — 167
July 17th—Words — 168
July 18th – Man vs. Prostate Exam — 169
July 25th – Happy Anniversary — 170

August 5th – Were Only Human — 172
August 9th – Overflowing Cup — 173
August 10th – NetFlixed!! — 175
August 16th – Peace — 177
August 24th – Namaste — 179
August 29th – Life — 180

September 1st – That's Love . . . . . . . . . . 182

September 15th – "Open" . . . . . . . . . . 183

September 20th – On the Move . . . . . . . . . 185

September 21st – "I WILL" . . . . . . . . . . 187

September 23rd – Tour Guide . . . . . . . . . . 189

September 27th – "Who Are You" . . . . . . . . 191

September 29th – The Seeds . . . . . . . . . . 193


October 8th – What is it All About? . . . . . . . . 194

October 11th – Happy Birthday . . . . . . . . . 195

October 29th – Where is President Obama? . . . . . 196


November 8th – Moments . . . . . . . . . . 198

November 9th –"Alright" . . . . . . . . . . 199

November 15th – The Same Boat . . . . . . . . 201

November 27th – LOVE & FEAR . . . . . . . . 203

The Miracle . . . . . . . . . . . 204


December 19th – "I'll Rise" . . . . . . . . . . 206

2020 – One Year In . . . . . . . . . . . 208


Afterwards . . . . . . . . . . . 209

Acknowledgements . . . . . . . . . . 212

About the Author . . . . . . . . . . . 213

Lost and found; by my side . . . . . . . . . . 214

I AM.
Happy, sad, good, and bad.


I AM.
Love and it's nemesis.


I AM.
Isolated though integrated.


I AM.
Many things at the same time.


AND.
Dearest to me is that;


I AM.


—


Andrew Smith

# INTRODUCTION

My wife, Janise Smith, suffered a massive stroke on March 18, 2019.

And what is a massive stroke? According to Heart and Stroke Canada: "A stroke happens when blood stops flowing to any part of your brain, damaging brain cells. The effects of a stroke depend on the part of the brain that was damaged, and the amount of damage done." A "massive" stroke means that a large area of the brain was denied blood. Janise's was an ischemic stroke, the most common type of stroke. It was likely due to high blood pressure.

**Janise Smith:**
- My girlfriend and best friend from June 1982
- My wife from July 1992
- The mother of our two boys: Jelani, born in April 1994 and Jabari, in August 2002.

Before Janise's stroke we were an affluent Black Canadian family with Caribbean roots. Janise managed the family and was always in the midst of organizing events to support the female movers and shakers of the Scarborough area of Toronto, Ontario. She organized the "Celebrate Excellence in Scarborough" event which honoured Scarborough residents, past and present plus she did a Big Mother's Day Event.  One of her biggest projects was "Be a Santa to a Senior", and she put in the same kind of endless energy and excitement into creating over-the-top birthday parties for the three men in her life (her boys and me).

Life was busy. We were not the traditional breakfast and dinner together everyday type of family. We had family vacations, always planned and organized by Janise, the family travel agent. We supported all of Janise's many functions as a family and I ran (and still run) a thriving accountancy firm. Our eldest had already moved out. Janise and I were right in the typical fast-moving routine chaos of a family with a school-aged child. Something was always happening or about to happen: there were Jabari's baseball games and everything around his schooling; business events; weekly movie nights at home; social events with our wide circle of friends and extended family; and family vacations. The burden of all the organization fell on the shoulders of Janise. She, the sun, and we the planets, gladly draw in by her infectious, gravitational pull. Janise needed to be busy; it gave her purpose and strength.

The universe has a way of forcing balance into life, often not in the way we choose or at the time of our choice.

After her stroke, everything in our lives changed. Our family dynamics and our individual and collective roles were impacted beyond our imagination. Starting with the crisis of finding Janise unconscious, the frenzied drive to the hospital, and then the uncertainty of wheth-er she would live, as a family, we faced what it truly means to love and back each other through adversity. Our extended family and our friends jumped in with their love and support.

The byproduct of this tragic event is this collection of notes. The writings of Janise's in-sane, devastated, sad, and lost husband. I had to contend with losing my best friend and my part-ner in parenting. I wrote these notes as a type of newsletter to keep our large network of friends and family informed in those first days after the stroke. So many people were asking for informa-tion that I could not respond to each email, telephone call, card, and text. I knew everyone was desperate for news due to how well-loved Janise and our family were and remain. I wrote these newsy snippets, and distributed them through a WhatsApp group, in my typical class-clown way; the humour sometimes serving to keep my own spirits up as well as those reading the notes. There was so much work to do; we had no time to wallow if we were going to rebuild Janise.

As #teamJanise swung into action, writing these notes helped me as it offered a place to download all the thoughts running through my head as I did the practical work of helping my ill wife and our sons figure out how to get through each day. I soon found that I was writing this on-line journal for myself as much as I was for others who wanted to know that Janise was getting the best care possible. Soon I found that the grapevine was in full effect. People whom I did not tell or had not been in contact with us for many rotations of the earth around the sun were reaching out to me. I also found that people I did not know were finding out about the newsletters.

Something quite magical started to happen. As I shared the story of our family, people would share their family experiences with me. The topics included illness but also went beyond illness to life challenges in general. It was healing for us all.

Our family's first year is similar to the first year of any family who finds themselves at the mercy of the medical system after an acute crisis. Hours before the stroke, everything was normal and all of a sudden, each day we were at the mercy of this report and that report, this medical specialist and the other. We were on a journey to reclaim our lives as our matriarch was no longer able to take care of us as she had for so many years; we had to become the caretak-ers. We stood confused and uncertain, looking for answers from the doctors, while trying to find meaning in this medical catastrophe and a path back to how things use to be, should be, were supposed to be. On this journey we found reflection, sadness, tears, humor, joy, laughter, and acceptance. We stopped taking our health for granted and changed our priorities. Health is now first. With Janise, I started a daily routine that includes exercise, supplementation, and the keto-genic diet with intermittent fasting.

We learned to be thankful. Thankful that Janise is with us and showing both the potential for and signs of improvement. Despite this all being new to us, we had to step up and become confident team members with our medical support team as we knew Janise best. We used what she loved (Caribbean music, tradition, and food) to create those "backlinks" to her past to support her where her brain was most devastated by stroke's damage. The **POWER** *of* **POSITIVITY** taught us that each day supplies us with a new sun and thus a new beginning. In our new reality a year later, we continue to push for more, as we move to the next stage of recovery, and the next level.

These notes are to serve as documentation of our path, our struggle, and our triumphs. They show a real example to others who, like us, were bewildered at the onset of a dramatic, life-altering illness. I hope as you follow our journey you learn lessons to help you with yours, whether you are in the immediate and sudden situation of caring for a loved one who has just suffered a stroke or you are some point between there and your new reality. Maybe you are a friend or family member and want to help but just don't know what to do: you will see how you can support a devastated family in these pages. I also hope these words will help you if you are in the caring profession and want more understanding of what it is like to be on the receiving end of health care services.

## *Have you had your Vitamin D today?*

# PART I

## All Hell
## Breaks Loose

# March 18, 2019

## When Things Fell Apart Things Fell Apart

Monday. March 18, 2019, at 2:45pm. This date and time now permanently ingrained in my mind. The phone call from Janise expressing concern: "I am not feeling like myself" and "I am seeing double." Her concerns made even more obvious to me as she was telling me this through slurred speech.

"I am coming home now!" I said and shot out of my office.

The drive home was the longest fifteen minutes of my life. I was having an internal discussion moving from: Janise is probably just tired; she works too hard. She's often up till the wee hours of the morning and forgets to eat to *this sounds like she is having a stroke.*

## What are the signs of a stroke?

**If you suspect someone is having a stroke, speed is key to effective treatment.**

**The most common sign of stroke are summarized by FAST:**

**F** – Face is drooping

**A** – Arms: can you raise both your arms

**S** – Speech slurred or jumbled

**T** – Time to call 911 immediately

**Some additional signs of stroke include:**

- Vision changes – blurred or double vision
- Sudden severe headache
- Numbness, usually on one side of the body
- Problems balancing

**Remember FAST.**

I weave in and out of traffic in my mission to cut the time off of my drive home. My mission is failing. I am in sync with what seemed to be every red light, stopped bus, truck, car, and pedestrian, each adding frustrating, unacceptable delay to the short drive home.

I pull into my driveway, jump out of the car without closing the door. I run, feeling breathless, as I'd been holding my breath through the short-long drive. I unlock and swing open the front door. "Janise! Janise! Janise!" I shout as I run down the stairs to her home office.

No answer.

I find her passed out. She is slouching in her office chair and the receiver of the landline phone she used to call me is dangling by its curly cord from the desk.

The "expletive" is real, and time is of the essence.

I make a frantic 911 call, where I am repeating, like a mantra, "My Wife! My Wife!" and the calm yet stern voice on the other end of the phone walks me back from the edge of that bridge, helping me regain composure. She tells me to check Janise to see if she is breathing, to look for other vitals, and open her air passages.

Jabari, our youngest son, arrives home from high school in the midst of the madness. "Everything is under control," I tell him. Then as the lady on the phone instructs me, I add, "Go upstairs and make sure the front door is unlocked for the ambulance and fire department. They are on the way."

With sirens blazing, a fire truck is the first to show up. They strap Janise to a chair and carry her up the stairs and outside to the ambulance that has arrived. The paramedics inform me that they are taking Janise to Scarborough General Hospital.

Speed, sirens, flashing lights...I did my best to keep up with the ambulance with Jabari riding shotgun beside me, but was stopped by red traffic lights, which thank God, did not deter the ambulance.

We are directed to Janise at the hospital in one of the emergency rooms. She is unconscious. There is already a breathing tube down her throat and the doctors and nurses are plugging her into machines that beep measurements of her heart rate, blood pressure, the amount of oxygen in her blood, and who knows what else. Jabari and I are directed to one of the waiting rooms, where we did as the room said...wait.

From here I make the calls, to our eldest son, Jelani, to my mom, etc. Everything is a blur of action yet all we can do is wait. Jelani and my mom show up and rush into the waiting room. We grasp each other and pray.

# March 20<sup>th</sup>

## What the HELL is a THALAMUS?

Janise suffered a stroke to both the left and right side of the thalamus (also known as the mini brain) of her brain on March 18, 2019.

This opened up so many questions:

* What does this mean?
* What damage has occurred?
* What is the impact of this damage?
* How will this impact Janise's quality of life?
* Can the damage be repaired?

      ...and first of all:

What the H, E, double hockey sticks (HELL!) is a thalamus? This last question is the only definitive answer that the medical minds can provide!

**What the HELL is a thalamus?**

This area of the brain is a hub which relays information / signals between other areas of the brain. Apparently, it is a very important area as almost every sensory system, but the olfactory system (associated with sense of smell), is impacted by this area of the brain. All of these functions and systems can be impacted by damage to the thalamus:

* Vision;
* Hearing;
* Touch;
* Consciousness and unconsciousness;
* Motor and language skills; and
* Thinking and complex decision making.

In addition, it is also integral in both short-term and long-term memory functions through its communication with the hippocampus area of the brain.

My response "DAMN!" with immediate regret for hearing this dump of medical information that I could not ignore or unhear.

The rest of my questions, for the most part, remain unanswered. Janise is in a coma, and the first step is for her to wake up. Waking up will be the first sign that the thalamus has some remaining function.

So, we continue to wait and pray.

# March 28<sup>th</sup>

## Until the End of Time

Playlist
### Adore by Prince

*One of our wedding songs (July 25, 1992).*

Janise is awake and in the Intensive Care Unit (ICU). She is making more and more strides each day. Full movement recognizing people, acknowledging people by their names, smiling, and waving. Initially they told me that they were not sure she would wake from her coma. We are amazed and stunned. Everything she does, since she opened her eyes, is a bonus. They have daily physio with her, assisted standing and sitting in a chair.

Her spirits are good. She is tired, of course, and is building up her mental, physical, and spiritual strength. She moves between an alert and dream state, with the states of alertness increasing gradually each day.

Time will heal her, and we are not in control of the clock.

I had the pleasure of witnessing one her vivid dreams last night where she was moving around and in full conversation. It is, however, one of these dreams, which in the past, she has on occasion woke up upset with me because of something I did in her dream!

... don't get me started!

Anyways! The nurses have hooked me up with a desk for my laptop, so I am able to do work and visit Janise at the same time (with free hospital Wifi!). The medical staff have been very welcoming to our family. It is understood that healing best occurs when the patient is surrounded with loved ones, familiar faces and ultimately familiar places. So my girl goin' see my mug ev'ry day!

Janise is getting excellent care, and I can't wait until this period in our lives simply becomes a story in the chapter of the book of our lives.

...from my wife's bedside,

Andrew 💜

# March 29<sup>th</sup>

## Pain

Pain is a necessary and inevitable part of life: it is our reaction that is a choice. Choosing joy and happiness in the face of pain allows us to grow, develop and mature. Undoubtedly, my family is in pain. I have been with Janise for 37 years. I must have been a wee little babe when we first started dating … yeah, I was a baby, let's stick with that story. We have 27 years of marriage, and two beautiful boys (Hey ladies! My boys are eligible and single for the right price—USD only!). There is so much more to add to our legacy in the present and in the future.

Great news! Janise has been moved. She is still within ICU but to a stepped-down unit for less critical patients, proving the old saying that "everything is relative," and that "less is actually more" (think about that!). The focus is now on getting her the overall rest she needs for her brain to heal. They are also moving her physically in her physio sessions during the day. We are looking to progress her to longer periods of alertness.

Janise gave us all a golden smile today showing that she is just resting and recharging before fully rebooting her full operating system. Can't wait to meet Janise 2.0; just hope I am able to keep up with her!

…from my wife's bedside,

Andrew

# March 30<sup>th</sup>

## "Can you Stand the Rain"

Playlist

### Can You Stand the Rain? by New Edition.

The words of this song ring in my ear right about now because it is raining what looks like a monsoon! I feel like all "this" is like a monsoon of medical jargon and confusion. There is no real certainty about when "this," like that monsoon out there, will stop.

So, what to do?

Put on my proverbial rain coat, boots, and get my umbrella (.....ella, ella, ella, eh, eh, eh eh...sorry now I got that damn Rihanna song in my head). Now where was I? Oh right, I was asking what you do if you are in a rainstorm. And the answer is get wet. You can start getting prepared, even to get a rowboat if needed. So, I'm prepared to stay here with Janise, and I have been sleeping in her hospital bed with her since she had the stroke. I have things organized so our sons feel fine on their own and others are stepping up to keep them company.

I know all of this too WILL pass as Janise is fighting hard.Trust me I know her. She is feeling all the support and love that each one of you have been throwing out to the universe with your prayers, thoughts, and acts of pure kindness. All the cards, notes, flowers, books, gifts, meals, prayers, visits, phone calls, and LOVE is what is keeping us going.

Today was interesting. The medical staff have been testing her with various questions to see how she is healing. She is able to recall the names of people that visit her; she does, however, get a bit confused on where she is and why she is in the hospital.

A funny thing happened today when the doctor asked if she knew who I was. Her answer: "Of course. He is Bodderation." Jamaicans, please explain the term "bodderation" to the non-Jamaicans LOL!

## Bodderation [ Bod-da-ray-shun] ◄》

*Noun*

A situation that is nonsensical to the point of being annoying.

*Janise and I at age 24, in the summer of 1990 at a friend's BBQ. Back when I had hair.*

I was offended by being referred to as someone who annoys or bothers people. This incident along with her being happier to see her sons than her husband has been added to a growing list of grievances that I will be going over with my wife at a later date.

BODDERATION! Well, I never!

...from my wife's bedside

Andrew 💜

# March 31st

## The Past, The Present

<u>The Past</u>

It was early summer of 1982 and close to the end of the school year. A teenage boy of 16 was throwing around a football with a couple of friends outside of his high school, his afro bouncing as he jumped up to catch a ball thrown to him. He sticks the catch and celebrates way too much, acting as if he just scored the winning touchdown in the Super Bowl.

As he throws the ball back to his friend, he sees a beautiful teenage girl walking across the street. He remembered she had attended the same school as he did a couple of years ago, back in Grade 8. He says "later" to his friends, runs over to the teenage girl.

"Hey Janise!" he says. She responds with, "Hi Andrew!" and as simple as that, their life begins together. He walks her home, and they never leave each other's side. The new couple spends every day of that summer together and become inseparable.

*Janise and I on a date in May 2017*

## The Present

It is March 31, 2019, and 1:00 am. That now "mature" man (mature is in quotes as this description is up for debate in some circles) crawls into the hospital bed of this beautiful women to support her and assist her in having a peaceful and restful night.

We have a view of the parking lot from Janise's hospital window. I show her the snow that is falling, late for the season as were almost into April. Janise wants out of the hospital bed and out of the hospital. She is squirming, moving to the edge of the bed and she turns to me saying, "Andrew, let's go!" I remind her that she is in healing mode and requires all the rest and support that the hospital, her family, and friends can provide. I tell her that the hospital is the best place for her at this time.

She is being restored through this process, becoming alert and awake for longer and longer periods of time. We've been told it will not be an easy road. Her recovery will be filled with potholes, but as the saying goes "if ya want good, ya nose haffi run!"

Janise is still on a feeding tube. It looks uncomfortable, going through her nose like it does. I am anticipating that this should be removed as soon as an assessment is made on her ability to swallow (note my maturity as I resisted a funny but obvious joke here! . Kind of proud of myself ).

So, we wait

...we pray

...we wait

...we pray.

Pray that the beautiful teenage girl that I reconnected with that fateful day while playing football with friends returns, restored to a

BIGGER!

BADDER!

& BETTER! version of Janise

....JANISE 2.0.

...from my wife's bedside

Andrew 🖤

# April 1st

## Competition

Janise the competitor. During the years, we have always had a "healthy?" competitive spirit in our relationship. This crossed over to all aspects of our life together, whether playing sports, wrestling, working out, video games, board games, card games, rock-paper-scissors, eating, and even the Olympic Sport – the dreaded staring contest: whoever blinks first is the LOSER!

Winning however is simply not enough. It is important and tradition in our family to totally humiliate, demoralize, and embarrass the LOSER for even having the ridiculous thought that they could possibly win the competition of the day. True satisfaction is achieved when the LOSER cannot even look in the eyes of the WINNER without feeling the pain and failure of the lose.

A little hardcore? A little too much?

Sure, but some fantastic memories

Janise was sleeping when I arrived at the hospital last night. She had a busy day, twice ripping out her feeding tube when I was there earlier in the day. In fact, we just gave up on the feeding tube thang as even with the hand restraints she managed to remove it, as well as the blood pressure device.

As I watched her sleep, she stirred and noticed me in the room. "Andrew, I want to go home."

I saw that fire in her eyes as she pushed herself up from the hospital bed into a sitting position and attempted to swing her legs over the bed to stand. I jumped on her (not in that way ... keeping it PG ) to prevent her from trying to stand which would likely end in a fall. The nurse ran in, but I told her "I got this." It was good old competition time in the Smith household—activity of choice: WRESTLING!

Janise was never one to fight clean. When I placed her back in the bed, I got agreement a verbal contract, (admissible in court) that she would not try to stand, take off her blood pressure monitor, or rip out her IV ... well, let's just say she was not holding up to the agreement.

There was no way I could allow her to win, so I pinned her. We were both laughing in the process. She tried to release her hands and to escape my grip with fake bites, kissing me to distract me from my task. The nurse was laughing and had a look as if to say "Wow, y'all crazy!"

At one point I was tired, 'cause the girl is TRONG! (note: in Jamaica, the word TRONG is even greater than the word STRONG). I used the old tactic of calling a time-out just to get a break. She would agree to the time-out, but then started to count down from three to start the activities once again. It all ended when she just got tired and fell asleep in my arms.

You know what that means of course... I WON, I WON, I WON!

But the reality is I know that Janise is the real winner.

...from my wife's bedside

Andrew

# April 2<sup>nd</sup>

## Dynamic Light

Janise was in the midst of organizing a community event and I had to let everyone know that it would not happen. I wrote this on Facebook. This event was one of her many networking events promoting and celebrating women in business. *Ladies Night Out!* was food, music, performances and included many women business booths highlighting their products

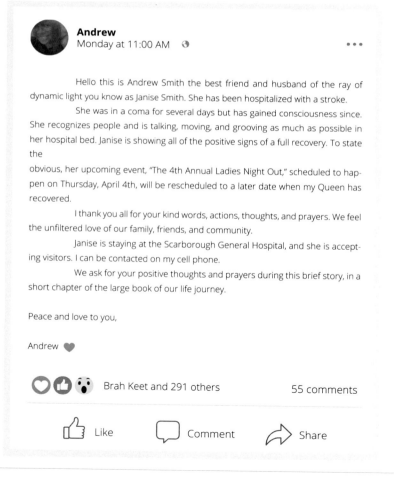

**Andrew**
Monday at 11:00 AM   🌐                              • • •

Hello this is Andrew Smith the best friend and husband of the ray of dynamic light you know as Janise Smith. She has been hospitalized with a stroke.

She was in a coma for several days but has gained consciousness since. She recognizes people and is talking, moving, and grooving as much as possible in her hospital bed. Janise is showing all of the positive signs of a full recovery. To state the

obvious, her upcoming event, "The 4th Annual Ladies Night Out," scheduled to happen on Thursday, April 4th, will be rescheduled to a later date when my Queen has recovered.

I thank you all for your kind words, actions, thoughts, and prayers. We feel the unfiltered love of our family, friends, and community.

Janise is staying at the Scarborough General Hospital, and she is accepting visitors. I can be contacted on my cell phone.

We ask for your positive thoughts and prayers during this brief story, in a short chapter of the large book of our life journey.

Peace and love to you,

Andrew 💜

❤️👍😮   Brah Keet and 291 others                    55 comments

👍 Like          💬 Comment          ➦ Share

# April 3<sup>rd</sup>

## The Brain

Playlist
**Three Little Birds by Bob Marley & The Wailers.**

The brain is amazing, but very much of a mystery. It has the potential to repair itself by repair-ing the damaged area or having healthy brain cells compensate for the damaged brain cells. Through healing, new connections are made. Janise's stroke left her with balance and memory issues.

I have learned that coming out of a coma is a gradual process. Memory gaps and lack of eye contact are normal conditions of the brain recovery process. Recovery can be assisted by familiar faces, voices, pictures, and songs. Giving the brain a foundation to reach back and find previous memories can help it to access, create, and repair connections.

"Three Little Birds," "No Woman No Cry," and "Redemption Songs" by Bob Marley & The Wailers have been some of the many songs that I have been singing to Janise in ICU. I am sad to report that so far, I have not been offered a record contract. Apparently, the ICU is not only a scent free area of the hospital, but also an autotune-free area of the hospital.

Your visits have been very helpful in getting Janise's mind active as remembering your names is providing Janise with opportunities to react and respond to your voices. I thank you for this from the heart.

Well, it is midnight, and time for me to sing "I'm Every Woman," the Chaka Khan version not the Whitney Houston one. The nurses in ICU really enjoy this set and my extravagant cos-tume changes. Time to work it!

...from my wife's bedside

Andrew

# April 4th

## Great Lessons

Before the stoke, Janise had always had a full plate on her hands and would not have it any other way. She is involved with many different organizations and groups; if you knew the extent of her involvement it would truly amaze you! The seeds she has sown have earned her the respect of the community as evidenced by the outpouring of pure love that she is receiving from those she befriended and those who relied upon her.

No doubt our family is experiencing the anguish and pain that naturally comes with the onset of an illness. We are also comforted by the love and support of the community that so relied on the hard work and good deeds of Janise. In addition, Janise's illness has become the catalyst for us all to pause, reflect, connect, and reconnect with others. To talk, meet, hug, cry, and laugh with those we have not dealt with since many moons past.

The medical staff is offering top quality care and they continue to be optimistic about Janise. They are happy with her progress to date as she is exhibiting all the positive signs of recovery.

I take great comfort in this, and I am reminded of the great lessons I have learned in my life as expressed through some old adages that I have picked up throughout the years like:

- "patience is a virtue"
- "time heals all wounds"
- "just give it time"
- "it will all get better in time"
- "it is not the load that breaks you down, it is how you carry it"

And, of course, the classic adages like:
- "expecting the unexpected, makes the unexpected, expected"
- "doing nothing is hard; you never know when you are done", and
- "alcohol, because no great story ever starts with 'you need to understand they had eaten sooooooo much salad.'"

Okay you got me: the last "adages" are not classics...LOL!

I got to the hospital late last night after a long day of working at my accounting firm after which I took our youngest to his baseball practice. Janise was sleeping peacefully, and I know that this woman's work is simply on pause. She will be back soon as energetic and passionate as ever. It is my job to ensure that she is working smarter  not harder; the introduction of balance will be the key.

...from my wife's bedside

Andrew 💜

# April 5<sup>th</sup>

## Medicine of the Past

Playlist
### Everything Michael Jackson, Ice Cube, Buju Banton

It was an eventful day today in ICU. Janise was visited by many loving friends and family from past and present, some of whose spirit we have not touched, smelt, or tasted since Moses was a boy!

Janise is receiving the best of medical care, but today I got tired of the traditional western medicine that she is receiving and tried out the medicine of the past. It was key to match the right medicine of the past with Janise's current condition. I searched and searched and finally found the answer: Janise needed "Billie Jean", "Beat It," "P.Y.T", "Don't Stop 'Til You Get Enough," "Smooth Criminal," 'Wanna Be Startin' Somethin,'" and "Remember The Time." If you have not guessed it by now, we were jamming to the music of one of Janise's favourite artist, Michael Jackson!

Nurses came in dancing and moon walking; we had Club ICU hopping. Janise was moving her head and shoulders, singing the words of the songs, and shuffling her feet in bed.

To be clear, she woke up for the King of Pop, NOT her husband!

To quote Ice Cube "It Was a Good Day!" Janise continues the trend to be more and more alert as the seconds, minutes, hours, and days pass by. Her voice is getting stronger, and her mind is getting sharper. She is still continuously ripping out the feeding tube from her nose and trying to leave her hospital bed, but it is this type of feisty behavior and determination that will get her better.


To paraphrase Buju Banton:

It's not an easy road. But we know Janise is on recovery to walk like the champion she is.


...from my wife's bedside


Andrew 💜

# April 6<sup>th</sup>

## Everything will work out

"Excuse me, sir!"

Whoa! I am awoken out of some much-needed REM sleep by the voice of the night nurse. I am a little disoriented and confused as I move from dreamland to reality. I examine my surroundings and see Janise in her hospital bed with the limbs of her vertically-challenged five-foot frame taking up the four corners of the bed. Our son, Jelani, is sitting in a chair beside me diligently typing away on his laptop situated on a portable nurse desk.

As for me, I start to feel the pain and discomfort of sitting and sleeping on a vinyl guest chair made from the hardest materials found on Earth. Yet the first thought in my head is, *I am with family.*

It is 11:30pm, the end of the day. Janise had received a number of visits from friends and family and is simply resting. She was sleeping for most of this day but had a burst of energy towards the end of the day when my god-sister and some old high school friends were visiting. She was attempting to communicate as much as possible, weaving herself in and out of conversations .

I got a flashback to when Jelani was a child and required surgery. At that time, he was in the hospital bed and Janise and I in the vinyl guest chairs, with Janise telling me, "Everything will work out, Andrew". This night as Janise sleeps, I am hearing those reassuring words resonate in my head: "Everything will work out, Andrew".

The nurse wheels in the most comfortable lounge chair (made from everything plush, bouncy, pillowy, and soft on Earth) for me to recline on and sleep for the night.

I comply

...from my wife's bedside

Andrew 💜

# April 6<sup>th</sup>

## Andrew 🖤

**Fun Fact:**

The 100 metre dash and marathon Olympic events are similar: each step will move the participant closer to the finish line. The key difference is the number of steps it takes to complete each race. Any race requires you to go one step at a time.

> Janise: get on your running shoes, do some warmups, stretch, and let's get to stepping. It does not matter which race we have been entered into, we still got to move to get to the finish line!

*... from my wife's hospital room,*

Andrew 🖤

# April 7<sup>th</sup>

## Thankful

Playlist
**"Be Thankful for What You Got" -**
**William DeVaughn - Release Date: March 1974.**

The message in this timeless tune directs us all to stop and give thanks for all of the things that we have in our lives, material and especially the non-material. Regardless of where you are in life you can still stand tall and work to get what you want and need. It is by no means a call to settle at your current location in your life journey, but to respect and to reflect on what it took to get you to this location, and recharge and reenergize for the journey ahead.

Throughout the day I received countless text messages from family and friends who visited Janise or were on their way to visit. On my arrival at the hospital in the evening I was met with visitors, and a batch of cards, handwritten notes, messages left with nurses, and even a certificate wishing Janise well and a speedy recovery.

I am thankful .

On the arrival of my brother, Micheal, his wife, Dawnelle, and daughter, Keisha, Janise woke up and found the energy to sing along to the Michael Jackson tunes I was playing. Not to be mean but it wasn't Janise's best performance—to be honest her voice was a little pitchy, but I let it go under the circumstances. This time...LOL!

I know I am wrong...but I am thankful .

During this time, on top of belting out some tunes, Janise engaged her brother-in-law, sister-in-law, and niece in conversation, correctly calling out their names and enjoying their company.

I am thankful.

During this conversation she engaged all of us in a sort of game of her own making that I can't find the words to truly explain. It involved some counting, multiplication, rolling dice, the number 24, and exercising...mainly arm curls. I am confused LOL! Janise grew tired after these activities and fell asleep. She had a full day! It was time for her to rest.

I am thankful.

More visitors arrived to show love and support including my god sister, Andrea, Ian and Mrs. Espinet, Uncle Keith ("Bra-Keet"), and his Queen Althea. They unfortunately missed the activities: Janise was out for the night.

I am thankful.

*If Love and Happiness was a picture...*

Bra-Keet brought me some chicken foot soup he made that was supposed to be for tomorrow's dinner. I will be eating it for Sunday lunch or maybe breakfast.... ain't no way this will last to Sunday dinner.

The time is 3:16am, the date April 7 and it is my birthday. I am celebrating this day with my wife sleeping in my arms.

I am truly, truly, truly thankful.

....from my wife's bedside

Andrew

# April 8<sup>th</sup>

## "Ribbon in the Sky"

Playlist

**Ribbon In the Sky by Stevie Wonder**

This song is very special to Janise and me. We so love the words and the melody that we selected it as one of our wedding songs for our July 25, 1992, union. The festivities of that date were a mere formality and public solidification of the real union and commitment that we made to each other as naive teenagers ten years earlier, in 1982.

The lyrics actually mirror our love for each other. Janise and I were always meant to be together. I am not a believer in coincidences, but believe that everything happens for a reason, and nothing happens before it's time. There is a life lesson to be gained from Janise's illness that I will leave for time to reveal. Speculation while we are in the trenches is a waste of the time; energy and attention is needed to get Janise to the goal of full recovery.

Janise had a fabulous day yesterday and in addition to my birthday provided our family with reasons to celebrate:

- she was alert for longer periods,
- communicating with visitors,
- sitting up on the side of her hospital bed with her feet dangling,
- sitting in a lounge chair for a couple of hours,
- posing for pictures and selfies with her signature BIG smile (some say her smile is generated from her soul; I agree!),

and of course breaking her promise/contract with me by ripping out her feeding tube.....DOH! There was non-stop food being delivered to Janise's room in ICU. The food selection included all of our favourites: curry chicken, cow foot, bagels, cheesecake, muffins, and pastries. I am envisioning these poor cows and chickens riding around in wheelchairs as a result of my consumption of chicken foot soup and cow foot this week.

Thank you for your support and the belly full!

......from my wife's bedside

Andrew

# April 9<sup>th</sup>

## "Stand"

Playlist
**Stand by Sly & The Family Stone**

**7:30pm**

I arrive at the hospital and Janise is sleeping. She is out for the night. She had her physio session earlier in the day and was sitting in a chair for about three hours. The activities of the day required some much-needed rest and recovery which she was getting, so, I let her be.

**1:30am**

Janise is struggling to release her hands from the restraints (the restraints are to prevent her from pulling out her feeding tube). I try to explain the purpose of the restraints to her, to no avail. Nurse Shirley, hearing the commotion, also explains the purpose of the restraints and asks her not to try to escape. She also failed to stop Janise's attempts to escape.

**1:40am**

Janise continues to struggle to release herself. It pains me to see this  so I give in and release her hands from the restraints. While holding her hands, I ask her, "Why are you trying to escape? What are you trying to do?"

She replies, "I want to stand!"

Okay it looks like this is happening.

I once again obtain a verbal legal contract from Janise that she will NOT pull out her feeding tube. My experience, however, with this specific verbal contract with Janise is that it is not worth the paper that it is written on! (Get it? Because there is no paper involved .....ha ha ha! Ooh! You're killing me, Andrew ).

I call Nurse Shirley in for backup. We raise the head of the bed up to make the transition from laying down to sitting easier. I tell Janise to swing her feet so that they hang over the side of the bed; she does and while holding my hands she raises herself to sitting.

Janise instructs me to turn around so she can hold on to my back for support while she attempts to stand. With Nurse Shirley behind Janise, and me in front with my back to her (and head turned backwards, like an owl), Janise attempts to stand.

First she pushes herself, maneuvering so she is sitting with her feet touching the ground. She then pushes off with her hands against the bed to rise to her feet. Janise is standing! Her balance is there, and it is strong. She occasionally holds on to my back to gain and regain her balance, but she is truly balancing under her own strength.

...Well, some shocking news to NONE of you: after Janise successfully stood on her own, she ripped out her feeding tube.

I lean on the old adage "A promise is a comfort to a fool."

...STANDING with my wife, from my wife's bedside

Andrew 💜

# April 10<sup>th</sup>

## Walking

Playlist

**Positive Vibration by Bob Marley & The Wailers**

The last three weeks have been an incredible journey of love and faith. Through the support of family, friends and colleagues I have seen the selflessness that exists within us all, and the unlimited potential and possibilities of our own humanity. I have seen the great power of being positive.

**CHOOSE ONE THOUGHT: CREATION OR DESTRUCTION**

Be intentional with the food you feed your mind, the thoughts you save and keep. Everything in life begins with a thought. With thoughts we only have two options, there is NO middle ground.

So yesterday, during the day, the nurse had Janise eating food by herself. Janise successfully fed herself liquids and solid food. Thank you, God, my wife can swallow!!!! (Now, for those of you who know me, take time to appreciate the double entendre of my last statement. ... Janise, when you are well and get around to reading this: I was weak and could not resist putting this sentence in the update. Alas, I gave into the great power of the comedy gods, and for this I repent!)

I digress.

Last night my wife and I strolled the halls of the Scarborough General ICU. Yes, Janise is walking!

I repeat we were walking through the halls of ICU: she in a hot blue hospital gown, and me in some old sweatpants and a long sleeve shirt. The ICU nurses and doctors were amazed to see us simply walking the halls and gleamed with joy.

We were walking and I introduced her to everyone we met.

Our minds were oblivious to the reality of our surroundings. We could feel the sand under our feet, the waves of the ocean that washed over our ankles, the extreme heat of the sun that beat down on our backs, and the gentle breeze that washed over our faces as we squinted to take a look at the sun...

WE WERE WALKING!

....WALKING with my wife, from my wife's bedside

Andrew ♥

# PART II

*Rehabilitation*

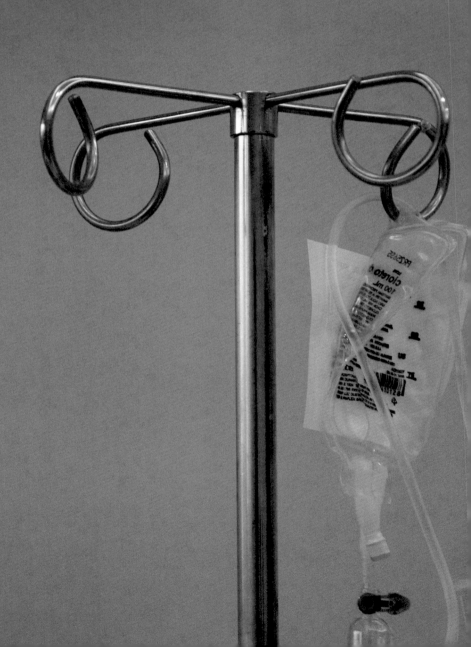

# April 11<sup>th</sup>

## Unplugged

Playlist
**For My Lover by Tracy Chapman.**

Janise has graduated once again. She has been moved out of ICU to a regular hospital room in the Scarborough General Hospital!

To recap her journey over the last three weeks: when admitted to the hospital she was comatose. PLUGGED into countless medical devices that managed her breathing and nutrition, and monitored her heart rate, blood pressure, oxygen in her blood, and many other things that are well beyond my crash course in medicine (via my Google searches).

Janise is now UNPLUGGED. Free to talk, sit, stand, walk, or just BE.

I do love the sound of a true artist shredding the fret board of an electric guitar and getting lost in the madness, noise, distortion, and energy. My true love, however, is when a guitar is void of the technology, UNPLUGGED, and free of the technology. In my opinion the experience of the clean, and clear voicings and rhythms of the acoustic guitar showcases music that is raw, unfiltered, honest and magical.

Janise is UNPLUGGED and she is magical. I have truly seen her raw determination, unfiltered strength, and pureness despite the chaos and disorder that we have experienced over the last three weeks.

We are now on the journey of rehabilitation which we will take a step at a time, and as much time as needed.

...from the bedside of The Lady Boss!

Andrew (Husband & Best Friend)

# April 12<sup>th</sup>

## Purpose

I arrive at the hospital at 7:30pm after a successful day at work. I met with some amazing clients, engaged in some deep, hearty, and meaningful conversations, provided some solid professional advice, and saved some good people a lot of taxes.

You know it is true: not all heroes wear capes. But enough about me, LOL!

Janise was in the middle of finishing her dinner and very much digging the hospital food which consisted of beef stroganoff served with rice and vegetables along with a selection of beverages, from orange juice, milk, water, and tea. I watched my beautiful wife enjoy the taste of food after being fed through a feeding tube for the longest time...Wow!

It then struck me! Janise had not cooked me a homemade meal in three weeks! I logically requested that she develop an action plan to correct this great wrong.

.... too soon you say?

Why my only goal is to get her well again and back to the routines that give her joy. (That just happened, epic recovery: from jerk to a little less of a jerk within two paragraphs).

I asked if she wanted to take a walk and she agreed.

The hospital gown that Janise was wearing was a bit tricky and prone to wardrobe malfunctions. I swear that it was designed by a combination Janet Jackson & Cardi B!

The walk was nice, we moved at a casual pace, unlike the hustle and bustle of our pre-hospital movements. There was no direction, no destination, and no hurry. There was purpose however in each step, as each step moves us closer and closer to our goal of full recovery with the added benefit of spending more and more quality time together. After all has been said and done, the only thing you keep from this world is the relationships you form and the memories you gain. This memory is a definite keeper!

We navigated our way throughout the hallway encountering hospital staff, beds with and without patients, other patients moving while others were still, and people with equipment looking for their next patient to probe and puncture.

The hospital was alive with that exciting nervous energy. Janise was soon exhausted. We arrived at her room, and I put her to sleep in her hospital bed.

...from the bedside of The Lady Boss!

Andrew (Husband & Best Friend) 🖤

P.S. La Senza has added a hospital gown line up to their next Fall Collection #ThisIsFakeNews

# April 13<sup>th</sup>

## New Spaces

It is Saturday, April 13, 2019, at 1:00am. Janise is sleeping peacefully in her hospital bed after a long day.

We have a lot to be thankful for as Janise is healing and rehabilitation is in full swing.

Last night she walked the hospital halls with her brother, Noel, and I. She is still building her strength so at times during the walk we drove the Queen around the facilities in a wheel-chair.

The highlight of today's activities for me was taking Janise outside beyond the confines of the hospital bed and the hospital itself. We went outside. Interacting with her in this "new" space was exciting.

She is now back in her room, sleeping peacefully in her hospital bed. Hopefully, she is dreaming of the new possibilities that are available to her. She is a stroke survivor but so much more than this limited definition. There is now a new and exciting path for her to take and define and redefine herself as she pleases.

...from the bedside of The Lady Boss!

Andrew (Husband & Best friend) ❤

# April 13<sup>th</sup>

## Familiar Truths

Playlist

**Be Careful of My Heart by Tracy Chapman**
**Atomic Dog by George Clinton**

Spent some quality time with Janise today on my hospital runs in between the baseball practice of our son, Jabari, and seeing clients at my office where I was preparing and filing tax returns. In my travels, I have found that there are some irrefutable and familiar truths in life, some old and some brand new:

1. The sun rises in the east and sets in the west

2. Gravity keeps us all grounded, literally

3. Once you come into contact with water you will be wet

4. Peeing in the wind will also get you wet

5. The Tax Man taketh away

6. "The dog that chases its tail will be dizzy."

(shout out to George Clinton's song Atomic Dog....

"Bow-wow-wow-yippie-yo-yippie-yay") and lastly

7. A ridiculous buffoon can become the leader of the free world

Janise had many visitors today. I sat back to watch her interact with her guests, smile that "sweet smile" with her guests, joke, laugh, and sing (with Ms. Letna). But mostly, I started to recognize the familiar mostly non-verbal characteristics that makes Janise, Janise.

The BIG smile with her trademark gap in her teeth (a beauty mark in African culture), the BRIGHT eyes that welcomes you into her world, the exaggerated facial expressions that makes you relax and forget your worries, and the kiss-teeth accompanied with the pushing to-gether of her eyebrows when she hears something silly or ridiculous. Janise is coming into her self and becoming familiar once again. Familiar with her surroundings, familiar to those who love her. But mostly familiar to herself.

....from the bedside of The Lady Boss!

Andrew (Husband & Best Friend)

# April 15th

## The Law of Inertia

In physics we learned about Newton's first law of motion also known as the law of inertia: "An object at rest stays at rest and an object in motion stays in motion with the same speed and in the same direction unless acted upon by an unbalanced force."

Things do what they do unless change is introduced. Change in the form of an un-balanced force. For example, when you pick up and attempt to drink your full (to the rim) cup of morning coffee , the coffee itself is at rest, moving zero miles per second. Our hand is that unbalanced force introducing motion to the coffee and spilling it all over our white shirt and lap!

Your natural primal response being "#!%$*!" (roughly translated as "son of a biscuit!").

Here's another example: when you are in a vehicle collision, your body continues at the speed of the vehicle even though your vehicle has stopped due to the collision. Thankfully, you WEAR YOUR SEATBELT (the unbalanced force). Your body is then stopped from continuing its motion at the direction and speed of your vehicle prior to impact.

My phone was blowing up with messages from those of you who have spent time with Janise while I was not by her side. These messages give me encouragement, and reinforce the fact that progress is being made.

A sample of the encouraging messages:

- "Janise has made so much improvement"
- "We sang "Redemption Song" together, went for walks and had a good time"
- "I came by today with my son, she had THAT SMILE going on; even for the little things THAT SMILE is there"
- "We saw Janise and had good conversation"
- "Just left Janise, Praise the Lord Jesus Christ she is pulling through and will be healed"
- "Andrew, Janise says your FEET are BIG and SMELL"

Hey! Son of a biscuit!  That's kind of personal  Too much sharing goin' on here, not helpful, not encouraging, LOL!

Admittedly, I am a little unbalanced  and one who enjoys stirring up a mess (a disturber). But now I am backed by science : Newton's first law of motion!

I thank you all for helping in the efforts to be that unbalanced force propelling Janise from the state of illness to rehabilitation and wellness.

...from the bedside of The Lady Boss!

Andrew (Husband & Best Friend) 💜

# April 16<sup>th</sup>

## Man Plans; God Laughs

There is an old proverb that states, "Man plans, and God laughs."

Even the most carefully thought-out plans are subject to the unknown. Whether it is unexpected changes, variables, and/or forces—the execution of our plans can turn out different than our original intent.

When our plans turn out different than our expectations, we immediately associate and attach an emotion to the outcome. The outcome is either "good" or "bad" and we are in turn happy or dissatisfied with the result. There are, however, good things that can come out of a bad result.

- ☑ Mental and physical strength
- ☑ Spiritual awakening
- ☑ Humility
- ☑ Improved relationship bonds
- ☑ New relationship bonds

The PLANS for our future were different than the current situation. However, our family has checked all of the above boxes from Janise's unplanned illness.

**I simply cannot resist checking one more box:**

- ☑ A belly full of home cooked meals

Thank you, your generosity is sooooo appreciated! You have stepped up to help our family. We are able to concentrate on Janise's wellness and I know that this is what our family needs, and in particular what Janise needs at this time. Just to throw it out there Janise also NEEDS me to drive a new luxury car like a Bentley, Porsche, or Mercedes-Benz. **

**the audience is silent, crickets can be heard in the auditorium along with a proverbial pin dropping. The author gets the message**

........okay, okay that was pushing it, I'll stick with your generous food offerings LOL!

The PLAN for Janise is open ended and flexible. It involves a lot of loving , laughter , tears , healing , holding , advocating , guarding, and protecting . The vehicle Janise is travelling in on her road to rehabilitation is filled with passengers who love her. They will bear witness to not only her arrival at the destination, but the spectacular journey that got her there.

....from the bedside of The Lady Boss!

Andrew (Husband & Best Friend) 🖤

# April 17<sup>th</sup>

## Happy Endings

Playlist
**Swoon Units by Digable Planets**

**My new normal:**

* Wake up with Janise at the hospital

* Take care of her in the morning

* Rush home to eat breakfast with our son, Jabari

* Drive Jabari to school

* Go to work

* Sneak time to visit Janise during the day, when possible

* Finish work

* Eat dinner with Jabari

* Play chess with Jabari

* Suffer a devastating loss in chess

* Listen to Jabari's recap of my devastating loss in chess (these kids today have no respect! )

* Lick the wounds to my ego

* Go to the hospital to spend the night with Janise


...........Repeat the next day


Time does belong to us, we are not it's victim, we are the master of time in our lives. Sharing and withholding our time at will, based ultimately on our priorities. The time spent with Janise, our sons, family, and friends have even more meaning and value than ever before. Although we are the masters of our time, we do not control how much time we have.

Now it is my time to take care of Janise, as she has taken care of me for the past ah, let's see, uhm...37 years!

Best memory of the day, Janise falling asleep while I massaged her feet.

Perhaps not the "happy ending" that I would have preferred in a previous time, but truly a "happy ending" at this time.


....from the bedside of The Lady Boss!


Andrew (Husband & Best Friend) ♥

# April 18th

## Pop Quiz·

"Okay class; clear off your desks. You will only be allowed to have a pencil in your hand. I will be handing out a pop quiz!" says the teacher, to which the students chant in unison, "Oh NO!"

What is a pop quiz? It is a short test given to students without prior warning. The teachers who engaged in this practice are not thought of in fond and glowing terms. "This is not FAIR!" is another classic chant of the students on receipt of the pop quiz.

Looking back at this "unfair" practice from older eyes, I see the logic in it. The purpose? you ask. Be Prepared to Be Unprepared (say it a couple times, it starts to make sense after the third time )

So here we are at the one-month anniversary of my wife being in the hospital (March 18th to April 18th). Guess what? I am not prepared for this!

"Oh No!"

"This is not FAIR!"

These hollow chants of my childhood give me no comfort, solution or conclusion to this Smith family pop quiz. I have however learned from the teacher that found the pop quiz to be a necessity in the learning process. Draw on all of the lessons learned up to the point in your life 'till when your pop quiz arrives. You don't know the questions yet, but the answers will come to you once the questions are revealed.

In the case of the answers to my particular pop quiz, they will be guided by the love. I have for my beautiful wife.... always.

....from the bedside of The Lady Boss!

Andrew (Husband & Best Friend) 🖤

# April 19<sup>th</sup>

## Dance

Playlist

**Pass It On by Bob Marley and The Wailers**

**Them Belly Full (But We Hungry) by Bob Marley and The Wailers**

We punish the child with an order: "Go to your room!" Nowadays we also need to take the added step of confiscating the cell phone, laptop, and tablet, in addition to disconnecting the Wi-Fi . We punish the prisoner by cutting their social ties to the world they know. We further punish them in prison by sending them to isolation. Cutting their social ties to the other prisoners.

It is evident that we are social beings, there is an energy that is created through the interaction we have between one another. This energy possesses the power to both sustain our overall health and heal our ills. We can truly help each other through the act of the giving of our time.

It is then no coincidence that many punishments handed out by our society involve isolation. Janise has a very strong group of family and friends that are providing the social support needed to cure her particular ills. We now look at facilities of rehabilitation to continue the journey to recovery.

What does rehabilitation look like? Unlimited possibilities for Janise. Through the support of her powerful social network, she will move beyond all limitations, whether imposed by medical staff, therapist, or Janise herself. We will be there to pick her up when she is down, and to celebrate each milestone she achieves.

Then at the finish, I will do the unthinkable: buy Janise some dancing shoes. FYI—buying Janise shoes makes as much sense as bringing sand with you on your trip to a beach: #JaniseHas2ManyShoes, #100sOfShoes, #SheOnlyGot2Feet .

But for her recovery, let's get the shoes and go dancing!

......from the bedside of The Lady Boss!

Andrew (Husband & Best Friend)

# April 20<sup>th</sup>

## Good Friday

Yesterday was Good Friday, a crucial day in the year where Christians celebrate when Jesus suffered and died on the cross for the sins of humankind. He was buried, later to be raised from the dead to life on the third day. Jamaicans give up drinking alcohol, eating pork, or meat altogether during Lent, and particularly on Good Friday. Hence the consumption of fish and bun and cheese is the tradition during this time.

A BIG shout out to friends for the delivery of delicious king fish with dumpling and bun and cheese . And my cousin for even more delicious bun & cheese .

In addition, a Really BIG shout-out to myself for exercising self-control and moderation, although coincidentally, they are on vacation during the Easter weekend.

Still, I proclaimed more than once, "Lawd mi Gaad, mi belly a bust!"

## Phrase: Lawd mi Gad, mi belly a bust!

*Translation:*
Dear Lord Jolly-Gee-Wilickers! I do believe I have consumed far more than my daily nutritional requirements

Janise had a great day. She was really UP, ALERT, and ENGAGING .

Jabari and I spent most of the day with her and we bumped into Tracey with two of her "pickney dem" (aka children) Nia & O'Neal (aka fried fish & dumpling—a long story) and Cousin Pam (aka Auntie Mom—a longer story!). There were lots of jokes, laughing, and an overall hopeful and positive vibe. Janise has come a long way!

Playlist
### Sons of The P by Digital Underground

Janise now sleeps peacefully, resting and mending, and mending and resting for the new day.

Blessings to you all

.....from the bedside of The Lady Boss!

Andrew (Husband & Best Friend) ❤

# April 21<sup>st</sup>

## Afro

I must confess that in my youth, it was all about the size, the girth, the volume, the mass; you know that tremendous, beautiful structure that I would present to those who showed interest.... I am of course talking about my afro—my hair! (For those of you who had other ideas of the topic I was leading up to, I will say a special prayer for you today as it is EASTER SUNDAY!)

Any hoo, my afro had to be BIG and round, perfectly round. In order to achieve this look, it involved enduring the dreaded nightly braiding of my hair by my mom (LOVE U Mom!). The braiding process involves combing out all the knots in your hair (Fun Fact: African hair is kinky and by nature knots up), then the braiding of hair into styles such as corn rows, bumps, or loose braids.

Oh, yes: Did I mention the process also involves EXCRUCIATING PAIN?!

There is the pain of combing out the knots, the pain of the tight braids, and to top it off the pain of being tapped on your head by your mom (LOVE U Mom!) if you moved or struggled during this torturous process.

But it was all worth it the next day as I untangled the braids, and combed my hair out with my afro pick (the one with the fist, my favourite comb) to reveal:

* The roundness
* The size
* The girth
* The volume
* The quantity
* The mass

Today is HAIR DAY, but not for me. Janise is going to get "her hair did." The day nurse (Carleen) has provided me with a list of items to get so she can wash and comb out Janise's hair. The list includes:

- shampoo
- detangling conditioner
- hair oil for African hair
- comb specifics which included the wide spacing of the teeth of the comb

You see today and for the last 28 years I have joined the ranks of the follicle-ly challenged. Where the beautiful lion's mane of afro once sat, there only remains the seat itself.... a very poetic way to tell you I am BALD! Bald, but not bitter; I save so much time now in my life not worrying about my hair. ***as the author writes these very positive comforting words, he wipes a tear from his left eye and dies a little inside***

So, I am GOOD! and Janise is getting the treatment from natural hair specialists NikandPea. Someone from their establishment will be giving Janise a fresh cornrow braid style tomorrow. Nice!

### Happy Birthday, Jelani!

A very special happy 25th birthday today to our son, Jelani. He is an example for us all. He has dealt with many challenges in his short life that would crush the spirits of much older men. It is evident that each obstacle that he experiences makes him stronger and he doesn't just survive, he has strived, thrived, and succeed!

Jelani, we love  you, are proud of you, and are excited to see the opportunities that you create for you.

.....from the bedside of The Lady Boss!

Andrew (Husband & Best Friend) 💜

# April 21<sup>st</sup>

## "Chant a Psalms a Day"

A BIG THANK YOU! & I SEE YOU GIRL! to Nurse Carleen at The Scarborough General Hospital.

Nurse Carleen stayed an hour past her shift to complete the washing, conditioning, moisturizing, and braiding of Janise's hair into Bantu knots. There are truly no words I can use to capture my appreciation for this high level of human caring .

**Bantu Knots Hairstyle Fun Facts**

Bantu knots were originated and popularized by the Bantu people. The name Bantu is a generic name for more than 300 ethnic groups that cover a large geographic region spanning from southern to central Africa. The knots consist of beautiful, small-coiled buns geometrically distributed throughout the hair.

Playlist
**Trench Town Rock by Bob Marley & The Wailers**

Janise saw many friends and family on this day, Easter Sunday. The connections, support, comradery, love, wisdom, jokes, contagious laughter, music, singing, and dancing have become expected, and the norm in Room 450. Beyond any narcotic, we are the real healers and pain killers for ourselves and those who are amongst us.

At times, I don't even feel that we are in a hospital setting, but the reminder of our real location is always present. This includes the nurses right outside the door, the cold institutional walls, the privacy drapes, the sign "Attention...blah, blah, the hospital is not responsible for patient items lost or stolen....blah blah blah", the pimped out hospital bed with the hydraulics, and Janise's hospital gown and non-slip socks (btw I need me a pair of the non-slip socks in my life).

Eventually the family and friends leave, tonight, I also leave, but Janise stays. Janise is in the hospital despite all the family, friends, food, and music that sometimes make it seem otherwise.

Playlist
## Chant a Psalm by Steel Pulse

A friend phoned me today with wise words and advice for some spiritual and mental healing. He said, "Go to the "Book of Psalms" and read a psalms a day." I said "Okay, I can do that".

So, I will do that!

.....from the bedside of The Lady Boss!

Andrew (Husband & Best Friend)

# April 23rd

## Women & Their Relationships

The hairdressers did a great job hooking Janise's hair up with a beautiful corn row style.

I walk into Janise's hospital room just in time to see the tail end of the creation/production of her new do. There is a small audience of visitors in attendance. We were all impressed with the final result!

Janise looks gorgeous! (....thoughts ran in my head of breaking her out of this joint and taking her home; if ya know what I'm sayin'!). Even a bald man like myself recognizes the importance of the relationship between a woman and her hair. So, I was happy that this task got done for my wife. Now that we are on the topic of woman and their important relationships, I as a modern man, also understand the important relationships that women have with a few other things like:

* Shoes
* Handbags
* Hats
* Wine
* Manicures
* Pedicures
* Spa days
* Eyebrows
* Waxing
* Threading
* Plucking
* Perfume
* Lotion
* Oils

(....the author needs to stop here, as although he may have ruffled a few feathers, he is not in that much trouble yet!....but sadly he continues ....)

* Discussing feelings

* Talking on the phone

* Talking while sports is on TV

* Talking while I am trying to sleep

(.....please stop him; he knows NOT what he is doing!)

* Being right!

* Being wrong and strong!

Playlist

## Can't Live with the World by Laura Mvula

The Turnaround

Now it is time for what we call in blues music, "the turnaround." The blues turnaround occupies the final two measures (11 and 12) of 12 bar blues. Particularly the 12th bar results in tension that sets up the resolution in the first bar of the song. Enough tension has been built up to this point LOL!)

But seriously, it feels good to have Janise's hospital room converted into a makeshift hair salon for a couple of hours for her to enjoy a much deserved beauty day. I am happy to have assisted in the coordination of this escape for my lovely wife.  My goal is to continue to pamper Janise and to free her world of stress as much as humanly possible. Her health takes precedent over everything. There is nothing so important in this world that is worth risking health. For without health there is no life. And now I am the gate keeper of Janise's mental and physical health and well-being.

.......from the bedside of The Lady Boss!

Andrew (Husband & Best Friend) 🖤

# April 24<sup>th</sup>

## Moving to Providence

It is moving day for Janise: the discharge has come through and she is leaving Scarborough General Hospital and headed off to Providence Health Care to continue her rehabilitation. Providence is well known for its rehabilitation programs and effectively transitioning patients of all ills from sickness to rehab, then to HOME.

My task this morning is that of packer and mover. Collecting all of Janise's toiletries, clothing, books, cards, flowers, phone, etc., for transport. It's hard out here in this world for husbands! However, we remain humble and thankful that we are able to assist the quality of our wive's lives forgoing our own. We also tuck our Superman cape under our clothing and make sure the BIG S on our chest is never revealed so as not to attract attention. (.....yea I hear ya: the last paragraph was a bit of an overplay. But if us men do not stroke our own egos, this important task would be left undone)

In between the packing and moving I managed to find some time to assist Janise with her care, helping her eat her breakfast, brushing her teeth, and moisturizing her skin with lotion after her shower.

My only regret was not playing some Teddy Pendergrass or Barry White as I applied lotion on my wife's skin and for those of you who don't have a clue who these PhD of Love Songs singers and writers are: SHAME ON YOU! My simple request is that you ask Alexa, Siri, or Google about these artists now!

Wow!

But Janise's ride is here now (the ambulance transport vehicle). Gotta get back to my husbandly packing and moving duties!

....from the bedside of The Lady Boss!

Andrew (Husband & Best Friend) . 🖤

# April 24<sup>th</sup>

## "Get Here"

Playlist
### Get Here by Oleta Adams

Overwhelming, drowning in the experience of it all. Not just the pain and the heart ache of the illness but also the joy and the healing. It is the unknown and the unwritten that brings both fear and hope.

The storm was harsh, brutal, and seemingly unrelenting. The memory of it is fading but that storm will never be forgotten. However, the storm itself is not the story; it is merely the background, a backdrop to the real story that is moving to centre stage. This story is one of goodness, kindness, selflessness, community, will, strength, power, and "over"standing. It is a story of beauty, grace, dignity, and love . The story of a mother, a wife, and a lover (Sorry to our sons for that last one—but nothing that therapy won't fix).

The REAL story is the story of Janise!

I am now left with a beautiful soul who has lost her way and is dependent on me to find her and bring her HOME.

Why?

Asking a storm "why?" will only get you one answer: "Because I am a storm, silly. This is what I do!"

"Over"standing

In order to gain knowledge, one must overcome one's ignorance. True knowledge of a topic, subject or experience comes from having the ability to stand over a topic and distinguish the forest from the trees to truly gain comprehension. We are machines of meaning and purpose and must take away lessons from our experiences. My particular revelation from this experience is the "over"standing of what truly is important in life versus everything else. I pray that this lesson will continue to feed me throughout the rest of my life.

Get Here!

We are here! We are at Providence. Now the work begins! What you lose in the blink of an eye takes many moons to regain, and that is why we are at Providence. To continue the gains from those who have expertise in these matters.

So, Janise lean on us ALL. We are the librarians to your beautiful, argumentative, stubborn, loving  mind.

Help us help you.

Guide us to you.

Let us guide you.

We are the light in the dark room, as you have been for us for so many years. Let us be the beacon of light in these foggy damp days after the storm has passed. We need you to get here period. No ifs, buts, or maybe's: just GET HERE!

......from the new beside of The Lady Boss!

Andrew (Husband & Best Friend) 💜

# April 26<sup>th</sup>

## The List

We are here at Providence HealthCare located in my neighbourhood of Scarborough just fifteen minutes from home. The building, staff and culture here give off an overall positive wellness vibe. The programs and facilities are in a word, impressive! The ceilings are high, the halls are BIG, wide, and bright. The staff are welcoming, pleasant, friendly, and accommodating.

When Janise arrived from Scarborough General Hospital transported by ambulance, within moments of touch-down, physiotherapist were assessing her: walking with her and asking her to stand up and sit down in order to determine her motor skills. The program was ON!

I was introduced to various members of what I call her Wellness Team, including a speech pathologist, physiotherapist, nurses, and a pharmacist. They asked a multitude of questions to really get to know Janise—not just from a medical-charting perspective, but from a deeper understanding of her lifestyle. The topics of discussion included work, play, family, likes and dislikes. It was a "Who is Janise? Session"! The Wellness Team were developing a personalized plan to get us back home, back to "normal." They wanted to know what "normal" looked like for the Smith family.

What will "normal" look like for the Smith family in the future?

The answer to the first question is easy: there is nothing "normal" about us—LOL! It is with the answer to the second question where the struggle occurs. This answer is yet to be known. We are currently in the process of writing, reviewing, editing and perfecting this script. However, I do know that the results will be EPIC!

OK going over my Status Update, let's see where we are:

- ☑ Arrival at Providence HealthCare.
- ☑ Andrew to select comfortable clothing, including undergarments and running shoes, for Janise to wear from her closet and drawers at home. She will be wearing her own clothing during her stay at Providence HealthCare!
- ☑ The Wellness Team is Engaged.
- ☑ The Wellness Program is ON!
- ☒ Andrew to understand why a woman's underwear collection is so vast and complicated.

Note: Andrew regrets including the last point in Janise's update

.......from the bedside of The Lady Boss!

Andrew (Husband & Best Friend) ♥

# April 27<sup>th</sup>

## "Alright"

Woke up this morning beside my wife in her hospital bed at Providence HealthCare. We got some good sleep; we need one of these beds at home! Now I have about three hours to spend with Janise before I have to drop Jabari to his baseball practice in Ajax: the countdown begins...

I show Janise the selection of clothing I brought for her from home that I neatly folded and hung up in her hospital closet. She selects her clothing for the day . Always helpful , Janise also gives me instructions on which of her garments (that I painstakingly selected through much consternation) I should return home immediately.

Fun Fact: Apparently there are some clothes that you simply just keep in your closet and drawers FOREVER and NEVER wear. In keeping with this logic, some of these very clothes even have the original price tags on them! Interesting .

Playlist
### Be Alright by Zapp

Back to the task at hand: I assist Janise get ready for the day. She brushes her teeth, showers, gets all lotioned up, and puts on her OWN clothing from her OWN closet. This is actually part of the healing process, as dressing in a hospital gown all day is a constant reminder that you are sick! Dressing in your OWN clothing gives you the vibe of wellness.

We pack in a lot in those three hours, from walking to the Tim Hortons—the coffee shop is within the Providence facility—for, yes, coffee, then I help Janise with her breakfast. We go on a brief visit to the Providence Internet Cafe and then to the Providence Gym (both on the same floor as Janise's room, while Tim Horton's is on one floor lower). Those hours went too fast and now I have "gots ta GO". Janise is tired from our morning activities anyway. I tuck her into her hospital bed and give her a kiss.

She falls asleep and I depart.

....from the bedside of The Lady Boss!

Andrew (Husband & Best Friend)

# April 28<sup>th</sup>

## Change

**Just Like You by The Brides of Funkenstein**

Change is the constant that we can depend on in our lives. Simply look back at your own life, as far back as you can remember to this very day. You have changed, from your childhood to now, and for you younger ones, even within your childhood. Everything changes: your hair, your look, your style, your weight, your eating habits, your attitude, your frame of reference, and your frame of mind. In essence, change marks the key events within our lives. it is the change itself that makes the events in our lives memorable. No change; will give you a monotonous life.

The life of the Smith family has changed.

Janise is the sun to the earthly bodies of Jabari, Jelani, and me. Providing us with the necessities of life to move forward daily. Light, food, warmth, joy, and my favourites: the heat and the fire.

It is true that the woman is at the centre of life in the household. She sets the focus, direction, and overall environment of the home. Janise continues to be this central force within our family from her satellite location away from the home. We are missing her guidance and direction though and this results in our feelings of discomfort and disruption. We are feeling arrested and seized.

This, however, is what change looks like, and change is inevitable.

Change then is to be embraced, held onto real tight and taken control of. Whether the factors that created the change are controllable or not, we must, as much as possible, take control of the results. Only then can we truly take control of our life. We are the active actors in the stage show we call our life. NEVER simply a member of the audience.

Janise it is time to raise the curtain: It's SHOW TIME!

......by the bedside of The Lady Boss!

Andrew (Husband & Best Friend)

# April 30th

## The Providence Routine

We have the Providence routine down now. We wake up, a hug and a kiss; no less, but sometimes a little more (but you didn't hear that from me). DAMN! I forgot I am leaving the very evidence to incriminate myself. . . it's actually in writing! Andrew, you fool!

Playlist
### Turn Off the Lights by Teddy Pendergrass

I assist Janise with getting ready for the day. Like a boy scout I am always ready and prepared to jump in and lend a helpful hand or two. This includes shower and lotion duties: yes, I know, and I'll repeat: "not all heroes wear capes". This one wears glasses and the occasional trench coat with speedos, but that's a longer story for another day **insert maniacal laugh and evil smile with the associated rubbing of the hands in circular motion!**

We eat breakfast together. I pick something up at the Tim Hortons downstairs and Janise eats the hospital food. Her breakfast today consisted of rolled oats, cottage cheese, whole wheat bread, one percent milk, prune juice, and hot tea. After breakfast it is time for our morning stroll on the third floor. Walking in a big circle past the gym, and internet cafe.

At this point in time sadly I must leave. We say our goodbyes, a hug and a kiss; no less, but sometimes a little more (but you didn't hear that from me). Janise starts her various physio sessions and I drive home to pick up Jabari and take him to school and then I go to work.

*Hot Pink! The wife and I striking a pose during one of our daily walks at Providence.*

Janise is improving both physically and mentally. Her progress to date has been nothing short of a miracle and we will be pushing for even more miracles in the future. These miracles are very much the result of Janise's strong mind, zest for life, and joyous spirit. Even when this thang had her in its full grip, she did not tap out.

She continued to fight

She continued to thrive

She continued to BE

She continued to SMILE in the face of it ALL.

Ladies and gentlemen, I present to you Mr. Teddy Pendergrass and his classic song - Turn Off the Lights.

If ya don't know, now ya know!

....from the bedside of The Lady Boss!

Andrew (Husband & Best Friend) 🖤

# May 1st

## Talk 2 Me

Providence HealthCare's official visiting hours are 24/7, 365 days a year. Very family friendly!

Not that any alternative visiting hours could stop me from seeing my wife anytime; however, it is good to know that visiting my wife at my convenience is encouraged and is not a thing to be dealt with between me and the powers that be. In fact, I have been sleeping at a hospital (Scarborough General and now Providence HealthCare) since March 18th! I don't know how comfortable I am going to be in our bed at home when we get over all of this. I am thinking of pimping out our bed at home with all sorts of hydraulics, flashing lights, retractable safety rails, wheels, brakes, and ceiling mirror just to get a good night's rest once we have to sleep back at home.

Ok you got me: the ceiling mirror is just something I slipped in for other reasons and may not help me in my quest for a good night's sleep, but you never know. Don't judge me! As I was saying.........I am gonna miss you, hospital bed, but I will be glad when you become a distant memory in our lives.

Janise is working hard in rehab, and she continues to make us all proud of her each and every day.

I walked Janise to her speech therapy appointment this morning before I left, and when I returned later in the day, she had just finished a physiotherapy session. She was tired, but her fatigue did not stop me from peppering her with questions.

Me: "How was speech therapy?"

Janise: "Fine."

Me: "How was physiotherapy?"

Janise: "Hard."

Me: "How is your day going?"

Janise: "Good."

Really? Answers: Fine, hard, and good (and the question was not "describe Andrew"!). No more than one word for your husband? I am interested in how your day is going! Does she not know how this feels?

The answer is YES!

We have actually just changed roles. How many times has Janise asked, "How was your day?" and I would throw a conversation ending one-word answer? They say turnaround is fair play.

Lesson learned!

Playlist
## Spacey Love by Rick James

...from the bedside of The Lady Boss!

Andrew (Husband and Best Friend) 🖤

# May 2<sup>nd</sup>

## Cold Shower

It was 5:40 am when we both woke up. I helped Janise get her robe on and passed her the soap and wash cloth. Janise likes to get to the shower early in the morning to avoid the line up from the other patients at Providence. She accomplishes her goal; she is at the shower first this day!

Victory!

Unbeknownst to Janise though, there is one key ingredient missing that will leave her totally unprepared for her shower.

HOT WATER!

Yea, Providence did not have any hot water. Apparently, there was some scheduled maintenance which resulted in the shutting off of the hot water.

"Wooooooooooo!"

"Aargh!"

"Sooooo Cold!"

and other hilarious shrills of horror emanated from the hospital shower.

Showing sympathy and empathy for my beloved wife's unfortunate situation, I attempt to offer words of support and encouragement. Alas, my attempts fail as I am overcome with uncontrollable laughter with tears flowing from my eyes. For some reason my actions raise questions of the legitimacy of my concern.

I know, eh? Ridiculous!

It all ends in due time, and we continue the morning routine. The highlight being our coffee date at the Providence Tim Hortons on the 2nd floor.

"Hey what's a nice girl like you doing in a place like this?"

I stay a bit longer on this morning and we have time to walk the halls after Janise eats her hospital breakfast plus we check out the Providence Internet café. In addition to the various computers within the internet café, this room has a mini library of donated books, old school board games, and various puzzles in process on several tables. Lots of activities to do in this room! I take up a book to read with Janise and just as we crack the book open, the speech therapist enters the room.

"Wow, I finally found you! I was looking everywhere for you guys," she says.

It is time for Janise's speech therapy. I walk Janise to the speech therapist's room, say my goodbyes, and give Janise a kiss. Janise has started her day, and I need to start mine. Time for us both to get to work!

.... from the bedside of The Lady Boss!

Andrew (Husband & Best Friend) 💜

# May 3rd

## "Everybody's Got a Thing"

Playlist

### I Got a Thing, You Got a Thing, Everybody's Got a Thing by Funkadelic

We are all so different, each built out of our own cultures, teachings, and life experiences. Yet we are all so similar regardless of the very differences that we take pride in that define us. Yes, all 7.53 billion of us who inhabit this Earth are special. Granted, some of us are more "special" than others, we are each special individuals with a unique perspective on life, illness, and our ultimate destiny: death and the afterlife.

So why are we here?

What is our purpose?

What is the purpose of all of this?

At this point, it would be great if I had some profound prophetic answer to these questions that would put these questions to rest; finally. But I got NOTHING.

Janise has two roommates at Providence who could not be more different from each other and more different from her. Yet it all works out, they have developed a real sense of community and social network amongst each other. They do care and look out for each other.

The 85- to 90-year-old African-Jamaican church lady who is heavily routinized. You can set the clock on her every activity in the day. From her strolls of the hospital halls to her praising of Jesus through song, to her questioning of God about her hospital fate despite her faith. She takes a while to warm up to you. But she warms up to you.

Then there's the 65-to-70-year-old European-Canadian woman. Always with a smile, pleasant and apologetic nature. Never wanting to be a bother, and grateful to have survived a stroke and aneurysm (at the same damn time!).

Last but not least, Janise: my ride or die who smiles from her soul and IS the LIGHT and ATTRACTION in every environment she enters. They each got a thing and put their thing together to help each other make it through each day. A helping hand, calling the nurse for assistance or simply conversation and company.

Perhaps this is the purpose of it ALL...to help each other pass the time before WE pass.

....from the bedside of The Lady Boss!

Andrew (Husband & Best Friend) 🖤

# May 5<sup>th</sup>

# Prevention & Rehabilitation

## Prevention

Janise's meal plan at Providence is labelled as the Heart Healthy Eating Plan.

The Plan overview is to:

- ☑ Eat balanced meals and limit processed foods.
- ☑ Limit foods with trans fats.
- ☑ Include omega-3 rich foods: fish (mackerel, sardines, herring, trout. anchovies), flaxseeds, hemp seeds, and walnuts.
- ☑ Include soluble fiber into diet: oatmeal, seeds, flax, chia), beans, fruit vegetables, and psyllium.
- ☑ Limit sugar-sweetened foods and beverages.
- ☑ Spice up your meals without salt (too much sodium can lead to high blood pressure, heart disease, stroke, and kidney disease).
- ⚠ Limit alcohol - "Houston we have a problem!".

Just kidding; yes, Janise does LOVE her wine, but for a long life, the above list is easily doable and achievable. Of course, I will support Janise by following these guidelines in my diet.

Prevention is key as the mere fact of having a stroke puts you at a greater risk of having another stroke.

## Rehabilitation

We have been provided with an "anticipated discharge date" of June 2. 2019.

When I saw this, at first to be honest, I had mixed feelings. I do want Janise home as soon as possible; we do, however, need to ensure that she is ready for home. I am all about the aggressive timelines and have set this date as the shared goal of Providence and the Smiths to welcome Janise home.

It is time that will be the ultimate adjudicator of the reasonableness of our shared goal.

Playlist

## With a Little Help from My Friends by The Beatles

Friends and family continue to show love in their offerings of support to our family. I am truly humbled by the many home cooked meals, prayers, and words of comfort. This is God's ministry in action, when we were down you stepped up, and lifted us up!

A special thank you to Ron Kharis for loaning us the tablet with the reading program that he wrote yourself! Janise and I had a great time reading the stories that were loaded on the tablet.

......from the bedside of The Lady Boss!

Andrew (Husband & Best Friend)

# May 5<sup>th</sup>

## "I'm Ready"

It was time to get Janise some Vitamin D
......from the sun! (aka Sunshine Vitamin) .

Playlist
### "Flashlight" by Parliament-Funkadelic

Not wanting to jinx the situation, but the weather seems to have changed. We were comfortably up into the double digits in temperature today and the sun escaped from behind the clouds. For the whole day everybody in The Greater Toronto Area (GTA) had a little light under the sun.

Fun Fact:

The human body is designed to produce Vitamin D when skin is exposed to sun light. There are many health benefits to the sunshine vitamin:

✔ Promotes health of bones and teeth

✔ Supports health of the immune system, brain, nervous system, lung functionality, and cardiovascular health

✔ Regulates insulin levels

✔ Helps with diabetes management, and cancer prevention

So, I changed our morning walking routine to include a walk outside, fresh air, grass, trees, park benches. This was a brand-new perspective for Janise to experience. She was now on the outside of Providence looking in.

This is a small taste of what leaving Providence looks like.

This is a small taste of what freedom looks like.

I capped off our walk by taking Janise to my car. We both sat inside my car, and I told her to get better so we can do this for real—with our only view of Providence being through the rear view and side mirrors. Janise promised to do just that!

On our walk back to the entrance of Providence and upstairs to her room, she refused to have me support her. She walked unassisted (I did however hover around her, but she did it!). We even took the stairs up to the third floor rather than taking the elevator.

Janise has come a long way and is READY!

Playlist
## I'm Ready by Tracy Chapman

...from the bedside of The Lady Boss!

Andrew (Husband & Best Friend) 🖤

# May 7th

## "Free"

Playlist
### Free by The Goodie Mob

Janise has a date of June 2nd as the date that she will be free to come home from Providence Health Care Rehabilitation Hospital. This has got me in the mode of examining our living space with a new eye. There are a series of steps to get to the front door of our home, and stairs to get up to our bedroom, and down to the basement.

Janise had trouble reaching the kitchen and laundry room cupboards pre-stroke, despite the towering five-foot frame she has been blessed with by her ancestors. Then there is her closet where I have been using a small step ladder to select clothes for her to wear during her hospital stay. Yes, there are a lot of physical challenges that need to be taken into consideration for welcoming Janise home. In addition to assisting Janise overcome the environmental and physical obstacles, my commitment to my family is to create and maintain a healthy, peaceful and stress-free world. This involves food, exercise and work-life balance.

Mostly, we will be avoiding things that appear in our world that elicit a reaction from us, but do not require a reaction from us.

We need to choose our responses or lack thereof wisely! I now use a litmus test of standard questions to assess things. It goes exactly like this (hit it!):

1      Is it a mountain or is it a mole hill?

2      If it is a mountain, is this mountain worth my time and attention?

3      What does success look like?

4      Does reacting or not reacting lead to success? ....and my personal favourites:

5      Do I even give a damn? And

6      Will anybody die?

(Please note that numbers 5 and 6 change in order depending on the situation).


....from the bedside of The Lady Boss!


Andrew (Husband & Best Friend)

# May 7<sup>th</sup>

## OK

"R U OK?"

The question consistently asked of people genuinely interested in Janise's condition is whether she is OK and is the family OK. The answer to this question is obvious to all parties: NO! There is nothing OK about this situation, yet I give a strong YES! This gives the other party involved in the conversation relief.

"That's great!" they respond.

However, the YES! I give is a genuine YES! The unspoken words that come after my answer of YES! As it is "in comparison to where she was on March 18th; comatose on a breathing machine and feeding tube."

So YES! Janise and the family are OK! I truly do believe that a positive outlook of all illnesses is a requirement of the recovery process. Our view then is always looking at the amazing accomplishments that Janise has made over time; this will inspire the positive trend to continue to full recovery.

Playlist

### Good Thoughts, Bad Thoughts by Funkadelic

As you can imagine, my life has been intertwined with the medical profession lately. Unfortunately for them, I am now an expert on all things stroke. I am basically a doctor now (a special shout out to Google Search: you complete me ).

I have met wonderful nurses, doctors, PSW's, social workers, physiotherapists, and speech therapists. Some of whom truly see their profession as more of a calling than a J O B. We have been blessed to have them in our lives at this time.

Fun Fact: The word therapist combines two words in the English language. The word "The" and the word "Rapist".

(Perhaps I should just get back on topic. Not liking the turn, I made down this back alley).

As Janise's advocate within the medical system, it is important for me to gather the information from the professionals (including Google: you complete me) and also use my knowledge of Janise with the lost art of common sense, to do what is best for my wife. In particular, pushing Janise past the limited expectations of the naysayers who flaunt the many letters that follow their name.

"A pleasure to meet you Mr. Smith. My name is Jane Doe and I am a specialist in blah, blah, blah. Please see my card and notice the 26 letters after my name (abcdefghijklmnopqrstuvwxyz)", they say.

To which I respond with my inside voice, "Dude, you just put the alphabet on your card, it means nothing!". We will continue to push Janise forward and plant seeds of 100 percent recovery in the garden of her mind.

...from the bedside of The Lady Boss!

Andrew (Husband & Best Friend) ♥

# May 8<sup>th</sup>

## Baseball Practice

It is minutes after 8pm and the temperature is around six Celsius and dropping rapidly. The air is brisk and there is a cold wind blowing from the direction of EVERYWHERE! This is relevant because I am outside somewhere in Ajax and it is feeling like Siberia right about now. I am wearing wool socks, two pairs of track pants, a long sleeve shirt, a sweater, hoodie, a baseball cap, tears and a runny nose, and regrets for not bringing a blanket.

Why in the world would I be outside on this night?

It is the night of Jabari's baseball practice with his team, The Stouffville Elite. This night is extra special because it is the first practice outside for the team for 2019. The grass in the baseball diamond is a rich green, a byproduct of the recent drenching that we have received over the last couple of weeks. But the grass and red clay within the diamond are dry.

The team is going over a series of situational game type plays, throwing, hitting and running drills. They are trying to wear off the rust accumulated from practicing indoors over the winter months. As familiar as all of this is to a baseball family, tonight something is off. My partner in crime Janise is not beside me watching her boy and providing much needed body heat for her MAN (if ya know what I'm sayin').

So, I capture this experience for her. The field illuminated by the lights of the baseball diamond, the fresh smell of outside, the noise of the baseball cleats mashing against the clay dirt, the crack of the bat, the sound of the ball hitting a baseball glove, the coaches' instructions, and the youthful enthusiasm and camaraderie of teenage boys. All these sights, sounds and smells cutting through the night. I will relate this experience in detail to Janise after practice when I am....

by the bedside of The Lady Boss!

Andrew (Husband & Best Friend) 🖤

# May 10<sup>th</sup>

## "Feels Good"

Playlist
**Feels Good by Tony! Toni! Tone!**

*Resting after one our walks at Providence.*

I remove Janise's tie-head (aka head tie or scarf) to reveal three large braids. I untangled each braid successfully and run my fingers through her rich thick beautiful natural hair. It feels good! I run the water on her hair and begin to apply the shampoo building up a good lather. Welcome to "The House of Andrew Hair Salon". Yes, on top of being an accountant with a CPA and CA designation, I have added "Sexy Hairdresser" to the long list of my recent accomplishments, which includes the title of Doctor (Google Search, you complete me).

It then strikes me, in the 37 years of being with Janise I have never washed her hair ...rinse, lather-shampoo again, rinse, then apply the leave in conditioner. The bucket list item for this body part has now been checked ✔ .

Fun Fact: This bucket list item is NOW closed; (ALL body parts have been completed).

The finale: top off the head of my Queen with the crown of a white hospital towel. Like LeBron James I have taken my talents elsewhere. In my case, to care my wife at Providence Health Centre. Not with the pay of an NBA star but more than matching the satisfaction.
It feels good!

My mom and I have teamed up on Janise's hair this day. She placed Janise's hair in the three large braids. I completed my task of washing, conditioning, then moisturizing her hair afterwards. Later today my mom will rebraid Janise's hair. Janise will then have her hair braided in a cornrow style courtesy of our close family friend, Jess.

It feels good!

Please note that "The House of Andrew Hair Salon" and the Sexy Hairdresser have only one client: The Lady Boss! Due to legalities, censorship, and confidentiality, the methods of payment have been removed from this document.

I can say that the payment received truly and always ....

Feels good!

.....From the bedside of The Lady Boss!

Andrew (Husband, Best Friend, Doctor!, and Sexy Hairdresser) 🖤

# May 10<sup>th</sup>

## Communication

Communication and its delivery are key to the process of collecting information. The body language, tone, rhythm, and facial expressions of the communicator are taken into account by the person receiving the information. They are ALL key elements that determine how the information will be received. The person communicating the right information in the wrong way may as well be communicating incorrect information as the results will be the same: communication breakdown.

Today I spoke with a master communicator who happens to be Janise's doctor at Providence. He reminded me of similar communications that I had with Janise's two doctors within ICU at The Scarborough General Hospital. The overall positive message of hope rang through loud and clear. There was an expectation of more improvements, based on the improvements that Janise has made to date. There was not the arrogant, dismissive, automated delivery of negative textbook "facts" that I experienced from a doctor within the ward at The Scarborough General Hospital, followed by this foolish admission when pressed by me:

"You know I don't really know your wife and I have not examined her yet".

Wow.

Thanks for showing up at your J O B. Please continue to act like a doctor. Quick question—is there anyone with *knowledge* I could speak with now?

A little harsh yes; but this is life and death we're dealing with. The "expletive!" is REAL! Janise's doctor at Providence confirmed my research on Janise's condition and went as far as suggesting additional websites that I could use as a source to do further research. Modern medicine has done all it can do for Janise at this point in time. Modern medicine had brought her back to consciousness when her brain gave up. Kept her breathing when she could not do it on her on. Had kept her nourished when she was unable to eat. Had kept her muscles from atrophying when she could not walk. Helped her use and build up muscle so she could relearn to walk. As this great communicator confirmed, Janise still has memory issues and balance problems. Her eyes are not able to move as flexibly as they once did, and she is not yet able to read text on a page. He added medicine isn't the way to fix it from this point forward as we have taken her as far as we can with mere medicine.

It is now up to the POWER of her brain to continue the healing work, and us—her family, friends, colleagues, and therapy staff—to assist her mind in creating and developing new neural connections to the CPU within her mind. We are witnessing the elasticity of the brain at work before our very eyes. However, it is our role to be active positive participants in this process. Our love  and connection to Janise will create more connections within her mind.

....From the bedside of The Lady Boss!

Andrew (Best Friend, Husband & Active Neural Connector) ♥

# May 11<sup>th</sup>

## Task List

Just woke up! It's 8:30 pm. There is a plate of king fish bones on my lap (it was NICE! ), the TV is watching me, and "informing" me of the latest buffoonery of our "leaders" as I sit in my "Big Daddy" chair in the living room. I begin to remember where I am, as well as my tasks completed and to be completed this Saturday evening.

I arrived home from seeing clients in my office three hours ago and put Janise's laundry from the hospital in the washing machine with some of Jabari's (including his baseball uniform) and my laundry. Jabari was out with friends playing basketball, so I had an opportunity to eat dinner and chill before doing some kick boxing exercises in the basement. Time has passed me now....but I got the rest that my body required! The Task List remains the same with some tasks being delayed in their execution.

Task List:

- [x] Put the wet washed clothing in the dryer

- [x] Check on Jabari (now in his room; he was kind/wise not to wake this sleeping GIANT)

- [x] Exercise while the clothes are drying

- [x] Bring Janise's clean laundry to the hospital tonight

- [x] Pick up Jabari tomorrow morning for his double header game

- [x] Spend Mother's Day (tomorrow) with Janise after Jabari's games.

Hats off to the single parents out there. To quote my childhood hero, Kermit The Frog, "It's not easy being green."

Earlier, I spent the better part of the morning with Janise. The day was nice and sunny so before breakfast, we were able to walk a bit of the grounds of Providence Health Centre where we stopped at park benches, read the inscriptions on various statues, and admired the green grass and budding leaves on the trees. Janise had been her normal happy self but appeared a bit more tired and groggy than normal. As a result, I scaled back on my grand plans to walk a larger area of the Providence grounds.

Cognizant of the time, I ensured that Janise was back to her room with enough time to eat breakfast, shower, and brush her teeth prior to her physiotherapy session today.

For now, as the wet clothing spins in the dryer, I try out some spin kicks on my punching bag, as the clothes dry.

...soon to be, by the bedside of The Lady Boss!

Andrew (Husband & Best Friend) 🖤

# May 12<sup>th</sup>

## Mothers' Day

It was so familiar; like old times again: Jabari, Jelani, Janise and I sitting around shooting the breeze, spending much needed quality time together. The occasion of this evening's meeting is Mother's Day. The closest men in Janise's life taking time to honor and respect their Queen.

Once again, I was reminded of the special relationship that a mother has with her sons. From the moment we arrived at her bedside at Providence to our departure, Janise was smiling from her eyes, cheeks, and mouth. She was engaged, conversational, active, reactive, and inter-active. We presented Janise with a beautiful purple card expressing our love, and our need and appreciation of her role in our lives. She LOVED ♥ the card and teared up as I read its contents to her.

We were in time to assist Janise with her dinner and spent the remainder of the evening after dinner watching the Raptors nail-bitting win in game seven over Philadelphia. We put Janise to sleep after a brief walk on the third floor, Janise walking us to the gym and church at Providence. It was time for us to leave.

Jelani drove to his home, and I took Jabari home with the latest batch of Janise's laundry as homework. I will do a load of laundry, then return to the hospital to sleep with my wife.

To all of the mothers: Happy Mother's Day

...from the bedside of The Lady Boss!

Andrew (Husband & Best Friend) ♥

# May 13<sup>th</sup>

## "All Day All Night"

Playlist
**All Day All Night by The Wailers**

The morning was busy at Providence. The nurses were hustling and bustling dealing with the many patients in their care. Changing patients and their sheets, showering patients, feeding patients, checking patients' vitals etc. They perform their duties in good spirits and with high energy! Through the organized confusion of this Monday morning, the nurses manage to maintain their personal relationships amongst each other; joking and sharing short stories of the latest and greatest happenings in their world. I am glad that I am able to reduce the work of the already overworked staff by being with Janise and serving at her leasure—you know: being available at Janise's beck and call.

Yes: Janise owes me BIG TIME! Trust me. I will be cashing in on this tremendous debt that she is building up with me (the accountant in me just will not let this debt go LOL! ). All kidding aside, my actions are simply the outward expression of the LOVE I have for Janise. There is no action that I can do that is great enough to encapsulate our LOVE-for one another.

I leave Janise this morning sleeping after our many activities of the morning:

1. Our traditional visit to The Providence Tim Hortons
2. Eating breakfast together
3. Getting Janise ready for the day (showering, brushing teeth, moisturizing skin with lotion, and dressing Janise in her own clothing)
So off to work for me, and dreamland for Janise.

....From the bedside of The Lady Boss!

Andrew (Husband & Best Friend)

# May 14<sup>th</sup>

## Appointments

BIG day today filled with appointments.

### Appointment 1

This first appointment was an oil change for my car. Unfortunately, I forgot to coordinate getting my summer tires out of storage so the winter tires will remain on at least until month end.

### Appointment 2

The second appointment is with Janise's neurologist at Scarborough General Hospital. I meet Janise and my mom back at Providence just in time (after being shuttled by the car dealership van) for the Wheel Trans pick up at 9:00am.

The meeting with her neurologist was both informative and promising. The last time he saw Janise she was in a coma with her breathing being assisted by a breathing machine and her nutrition being received through a feeding tube. He performed various cognitive and motor tests on Janise and went over in detail the impact of the stroke on Janise. He was surprised and encouraged at her progress and reiterated that:

1 ."These are early days", and

2. "Stroke recovery can occur up to one year after the actual stroke."

Now we know for sure that we have been involuntarily entered into a marathon as opposed to a sprint. There were many BIG complicated five-dollar words thrown around at the meeting, but the neurologist was able to keep up with my vocabulary. I am now a Doctor! (Thank you, Google!)

**Appointment 3**

This third and final appointment was more of a group meeting this time at Providence. Janise and I joined by Janise's speech therapist, social worker, physiotherapist, and occupational therapist. This meeting and the previous meeting with the neurologist had similar themes and were consistent with my personal assessment of Janise's current condition. There are some really good signs of progress, but Janise does suffer from confusion as a result of the damage to the thalamus area of her brain (the area that receives and sends signals throughout the brain).

This meeting was more focused on what her day-to-day needs are right now. We ended this meeting with all in the room in agreement with my request to bring Janise home for the long weekend (Saturday afternoon to Tuesday morning). We agreed to get Janise in truly familiar settings to see how she reacts and improves in this environment. We have already had almost two months of her being institutionalized in a hospital and now in a rehab hospital; let's see what the medicine of HOME does for her overall health and well-being.

There is truly no place like HOME!

....From the bedside of The Lady Boss!

Andrew (Husband and Best Friend) 🖤

# May 15<sup>th</sup>

## Time

It is a limited commodity that we cannot create or duplicate. It is often wasted or simply thrown away. The young have too much of it, and the old need more of it. It moves too slow when you are young, and speeds up to lightning speeds as you age.

Playlist
**No Time to Play by Guru**

Every second, minute, hour, day, week, month and year is measured consistently. They each take up the same TIME as they always have. Hence it is our perception of TIME that changes with TIME.

Our family situation has altered my perception and has necessitated my need to take full ownership and control of my TIME. The moments spent with the people in my life are no longer taken for granted. There is the realization that nothing is guaranteed, and that things change in the blink of an eye.

The moments spent with Janise from our talks, walks, meals, medical appointments, to simply sleeping together in each other's arms are special. TIME spent away from loved ones through work, rest, or play has been re-evaluated as either being required or NOT.

One guess: How much TIME do I now spend on things that are NOT required?

If you guessed ZERO you are correct!

...from the bedside of The Lady Boss!

Andrew (Husband & Best Friend) ♥

# May 16th

## Fuel for the Tank

Today I was seeing two of my favourite clients (BIG shout out to Lori & Katie!). I always look forward to this visit as the experience always fills me up with positive energy. Nowadays my tank requires a constant fueling of positive vibrations of which Treasure Island Toys has an infinite supply! We get the work done and have fun at the same time; this is actually my expectation everywhere especially at this spectacular specialty toy store on the Danforth in Toronto.

### Hidden in Plain Sight

I head outside at one point to top up the parking meter on the Danforth where I am parked. I bump into this lovely young millennial couple. The couple looks confused. They look down at their phone, then at the parking meter. They repeat this action several times in hopes that it will resolve their problem. It does not seem to be working.

I walk up to the couple my hands full of loonies, toonies, quarters, dimes, and nickels ready to feed the parking meter. "You kids are looking at your phone for answers" I say, then show them my hand full of change. "This is the answer to your problem, old school!"

They laugh and admit that they have no physical money for parking. I go up to the parking meter and put a quarter in the machine. It rejects my quarter and spits it out into the change tray.

Now we are all confused!

I open the change tray and it reveals a beautiful sight: eight dollars in change! (Thank you, baby Jesus!) I turn to the couple and say, "Y'all were looking at your phone and the answer was hidden in plain sight right in front of you, inside the parking meter change tray." I go on, "now I am rich, and you are not!"

The young lady turns to me and says, "well, at least pay for one hour of our parking for us." I agree and put three dollars of this found money in the parking meter for an hour of parking for my "new friends." They are thankful, and I am thankful. I have actually filled this couple's tank with some of the positive vibrations that were passed on to me from Treasure Island Toys.

I then feed the parking meter for my car and head back to the store.

Lessons learned: check every parking meter on the Danforth! I have done better on these machines than any casino I've ever been to.

Seriously though, technology is great; it is our friend. However, let's not overlook our real physical environment that we actual exist within. It is the physical environment of our HOME  that I will be bringing Janise to this weekend.

I look at the experience with my "new friends" as an omen. The cure for Janise is hidden in plain sight. It is within the very environment in which we both call HOME.

....from the bedside of the Lady Boss!

Andrew (Husband & Best Friend) 🖤

# May 19<sup>th</sup>

## Game Day

Yesterday was Saturday May 18, 2019. This day has a tremendous amount of significance; it is exactly two months to the day that Janise suffered a stroke. It is also the day that I sprung Janise out of Providence Health Care for the long weekend: Saturday afternoon to Tuesday morning.

I dropped Jabari to his baseball game in the West end and arrived at Providence to pick up Janise a little after 12:15pm. Janise was finishing up her lunch, so it gave me the opportunity to pack her bags for our weekend escape. While packing Janise's bags, a nurse, who requires all to call her "The Beautiful Rachel" met with me to provide me with my weekend instructions.

Fun Fact: "The Beautiful Rachel" is actually beautiful. She is a jovial, professional, and dedicated 47-year-old Jamaican Canadian nurse. She uses the Jamaican culture of fun, humor and music on her patients to help them get through their day. She is very much a character out of the mind of the Jamaican playwright Oliver Samuels. Unfortunately, "The Beautiful Rachel's" partner in crime, Nurse "Big Batty Marcia," was not working this weekend to see Janise off.

The hospital release papers are signed, bags a packed, and I am rolling Janise out of her room in a medical four-wheel rollator (one of those walkers for stroke victims that you can also use as a wheel chair). As we are leaving the room, Janise's face lights up. Her massive smile illuminates the room. She then does her best impression of the stiff, royal wave to her loyal subjects who include her roommates, nurses, staff, and visitors; frankly, everyone we passed leaving Providence.

On reflection Saturday, May 18th was a 180 degree change from Monday, March 18th. It was Jabari's game day (where his team played a double header) to see how he would perform with the added pressure of his mother in the stands cheering him on. It was Janise's game day to see how she would react in the real world. It was my game day to see if I can take care of Janise outside of the walls and support of an institution.

We all stepped up to the plate, took a swing, connected, ran the bases and were safe!

1. Jabari hit for a triple in one of his games!

2. Janise cheered for her boy!

3. Later enjoyed the company of family at home with the bonus of a delicious dinner prepared by our niece "The Beautiful & Talented" Paida.

4. I did not break Janise (the double entendre is intentional! ).

....from our Home

Andrew (Husband & Best Friend) 💜

# May 20<sup>th</sup>

## The Long Weekend

Historically, the "three-day weekend" always seems to go by way too fast. This particular long weekend seemed to pass by even faster than normal.

Our weekend HOME with Janise was amazing! It included:

* Watching our son play baseball;
* Spending time with family and friends;
* Cooking breakfast, lunch and dinner;
* Dancing and singing;
* Watching the fireworks ;
* A whole lot of tears ;
* A whole lot of laughter ;
* A whole lot of LOVE ; and
* Rest & relaxation.

I must be honest and reveal that there were some #metoo moments that occurred over our time together. However, I have informed the authorities to drop all charges against Janise, as I will not be moving forward with legal action .

Fun Fact: The symbol "#" was referred to as the term "Pound" while I was growing up. In today's twitter generation it is now referred as a "Hashtag". #metoo would have a bit of a different meaning in the pre-twitter world .

The highlight of our day today was our impromptu dance party. We started off dancing and singing to Mary J. Blige's first album - What's the 411? This is one of Janise's favourite albums, she knows all of the lyrics to each song. Dancing has enabled Janise to regain control of the co-ordination of her limbs and to regain her balance while on her feet.

During our dance party we were joined by our niece and her fiancé. The young couple did their thing and kept the pace up with our old school party, introducing some new school moves to our fete. At one point we traded dancing to each other's wedding songs: the song for their upcoming wedding is the Ed Sheeran song, "Perfect;" our wedding song was Stevie Wonder's song, "Ribbons in the Sky."

With Shamiso & Luckner:

We danced

We sang

We laughed

We talked

There were deep conversations

There were tears

There was time  shared

There was LOVE shared

For this we are thankful & blessed!

Our day ended watching some of the fireworks at a Scarborough Park and returning home to sleep. Janise will return to Providence tomorrow morning. I will be bringing Janise home each weekend up to her discharge date of June 2nd.

...from our HOME

Andrew (Husband & Best Friend) 💜

# May 22<sup>nd</sup>

## Back 2 the Future

Things from our past often get recycled and repackaged and pop up into our present and future. Hence the sayings:

"If you do not know where you come from, then you don't know where you are, and if you don't know where you are, then you don't know where you're going."

and

"those who do not know their past are condemned to repeat it"

It was time to take Janise back to Providence HealthCare after an amazing long weekend at HOME.

It is bittersweet.

On the morning of May 21st we get ready for the day, Janise's brother, Noel, is present to see his sister and lend a helping hand. Jabari is ready. It is time to drop Jabari to school and Janise back to Providence.

I drive the group down the same path Janise would drive to drop our son to school each morning.

It is so familiar to Janise. She points out the various grocery stores, fast food chains, gas stations, mom and pop stores, and other businesses that have not paid me for advertising so they will remain nameless in this update.

Her mind is really working and connecting to these surroundings:

* They are familiar;
* They are comforting;
* They are an integral part of her past.

They are now being reconnected to her present.

Janise notices the new construction that has jumped up since she has been in captivity. Kingston Road is losing its historic pay-by-the-hour motels, replacing them with new condominium construction. Wow! First General Motors shuts down their operations in Oshawa, and now the ladies of the night have less venues from which to work. This economy is killing everyone!

We arrive at Jabari's school, say our goodbyes, and then we are off to Providence to drop Janise off. It was a struggle to convince Janise to get out of the car and return to her room in Providence.

Heart Breaking.
The struggle was real.
She was finally convinced by my reassurance that I would be seeing her in the evening as she sees me every evening, and the fact that I will be picking her up Thursday evening to attend the wedding of our niece on Friday. Her brother and I WALKED with Janise back into Providence, took the elevator up to the third floor, then WALKED with Janise to her room.

The nurses, staff, patients, and her roommates were elated to see Janise. The Queen had arrived at Providence and again, did her stiff royal wave to greet her subjects.
God bless Queen Janise.

...from the bedside of The Lady Boss!

Andrew (Husband & Best Friend) 🖤

## Home 4 the Weekend

It is 7 pm. Jabari is in his room doing homework. The pork back ribs have been washed with vinegar, seasoned, and are in the roasting pan within the oven set at a temperature of 350 degrees. There is a pot of water on the stove (set at high) waiting for brown rice to be dumped in once the water starts to boil. Sliced avocados and beets have been prepared and are in the fridge ready to join the ribs and the rice for dinner. The smell of dinner cooking starts to emanate from the kitchen.

The TV is blaring some random show and Janise is quizzing me:

Where is Jelani?

At work

What is Jabari doing?

Homework in his room

What are you doing?

Cooking dinner, Officer!
I mean Janise 😵

What are you cooking?

Pork & brown rice

We R Home 🖤 once again. 😵

There was a lot of anticipation for this moment, this second weekend HOME. Janise had both the speech therapist at Providence and my mother (visiting Janise at Providence) call me throughout the day. She would come on the phone to remind me to pick her up and find out my latest ETA.

Now We R Home ❤ once again.

...from HOME

Andrew (Husband & Best Friend) ❤

# May 25<sup>th</sup>

## Shamiso's Wedding

*Enjoying Shamiso's wedding day.*

Saturday, May 25th - 8am. It is 11 Celsius and approximately a 110% chance of rain, as it is pouring rain!

We just dropped Jabari off at the Pan Am baseball complex in Ajax for his game at 9 am. Given the current conditions there is a 110% chance that all of his games today will be rained out. But we go through the motions and wait for the official notice from the geniuses in charge. Janise and I remain dry and warm in the car and Jabari is in the midst of the pleasantries outside. Janise is exhausted and sleeps in the passenger seat as I write.

We had an amazing time at the wedding of our niece, Shamiso, and her fiancé, Luckner. The intimate ceremony took place outside in a covered space with the backdrop of a luscious green park and the lake. Nerves were on high alert as Luckner dropped the wedding ring that he was to place on his anxious bride's finger. However, like a champ he recovered, made light of the situation, and completed his task: they are now ONE.

The events that followed included the wedding traditions of pictures, connecting and reconnecting with new and old family members, food, speeches, lots of dancing, and lots of Beyonce music. Shamiso is obsessed with Beyonce! The Beehive was in the house.

The attendees of the wedding travelled many hours and days to see this beautiful union, the places they came from include:
* Zimbabwe;
* Nigeria;
* Peterborough;
* Oshawa; and
* Toronto - (a special mention to my girl Straight Outta Providence!).

Janise hit the dancefloor like it was nobody's business! Shakin', clappin', steppin', slidin', whinin', and grindin'.....GOOD TIMES!

*Grooving at our niece and nephew-in-law's wedding*

Someone explain to me why she is still unbalanced while simply walking when she can dance like that!? Perhaps the solution is to turn walking into a dance with theme music for Janise. Yes!

Well it is still raining, and it is past game time for Jabari. Wait! I think I just saw...wait... could it be

....yes...

My GOD!

IT'S NOAH'S ARK!

The geniuses have now called the game and all the games for today. We are headed home.

....from wet Ajax

Andrew (Husband & Best Friend) ❤

# May 25<sup>th</sup>

## Advice for the Young Couple

Love 🖤 & Marriage

Chapter One, Page One & Sentence One

(The ONE RULE aka One, One, One)


.....advice to the young couple who just got married.

There is nothing more funny, sad, humbling, ridiculous, insane, or unexplainable than REAL Life. It will continue to amaze you throughout the years with each new experience. The new "normals", the new highs, and the new not-so-highs. What's most important is the experience itself with the associated lessons. Unfortunately, not all of the lessons are crystal clear.


....and the point then? You ask?


The point then is simply to experience it together and get through it together!

Sometimes the point is the experience itself, as each experience will add yet another brick to the solid foundation of your relationship. Giving it the strength needed to stand, survive and to thrive!


Remember you are ONE!


...from Aunt Janise & Uncle Andrew with 🖤

# May 27<sup>th</sup>

## Living 4 the Weekend!

Having Janise HOME for the second weekend in a row was NICE!

Busy Weekend!

My brother-in-law, Noel, stepped up beyond the call of duty for his sister. From helping to repair a shower leak so that Janise is able to use the stand-up shower in our bathroom, to helping me clear up and move Janise's basement office to the main floor. Most of this was done after watching the dynamic Toronto Raptors series win over the Milwaukee Bucks. Let's just say we stayed up from Saturday night to way past sunrise on Sunday.

Thank you, BROTHER! Thank you also to Tracey Brissett-Grose for dropping off a beautiful flower box for our porch and helping to plant some flowers in our garden. Thank you, SISTER!

Janise has been progressing, almost forcing herself to wellness. Discouraging me from holding her or hovering around her while she walks. She enjoyed going grocery shopping with me and I got a good workout running up to catch her and our shopping cart throughout our trip. My greatest fear of Janise falling in the grocery store was not realized. I prefer having wifey around, more than the millions of dollars that I would surely secure from the slip and fall lawsuit.

**LOVE 💜 over MONEY ALWAYS!**

We took time over the weekend to read the many get well cards that Janise received over the last two months. She read them multiple times and enjoyed each and every one of them—overwhelmed with the LOVE and support that everyone has expressed.

Today, we get a 28-day Holter for Janise, a portable device which monitors her ECG activity. Janise's neurologist is still trying to figure out why her stroke happened as there were no signs of stroke before her stroke occurred or subsequent to this traumatic event. Let's see if our modern medicine can solve this puzzle.

I drop Janise off at Providence and head downtown for some meetings. I will return to be with my wife in the evening and best of all, break her out of this joint permanently on Thursday evening.

We Are Ready!

...from the bedside of The Lady Boss!

Andrew (Husband & Best Friend) 💜

# May 28th

## "Count the Days"

Playlist
### Count the Days by Prince

It is 5am. Adele, Janise's lovely 92-year-old German roommate has been struggling to sleep all night. Her asthma has been acting up, and she is coughing and wheezing.

I checked up on her throughout the night as Linda (Janise's other roommate) and Janise are locked in their individual dream worlds; not impacted by Adele's struggles. Adele and I have had some good, deep, and personal conversations about life, marriage, children, sickness—you name it! Adele has earned knowledge, wisdom and understanding all paid for with every wrinkle and gray hair she owns.

We are of different races, cultures, backgrounds, and backstories yet we share many of the same life experiences. The human story is the same. We need to learn this lesson while we are all NOT battling sickness, as this is the true fix for the human condition. Unfortunately, the politics of separation which is the mask of greed, power, and control rules the day.

I get up to assist Adele, pour some water for her to drink, and offer her my ears. She tells me she is headed home today, and I am happy for her. She no longer needs to count the days at Providence as the day is here!

I go back to sleep with Janise, but something is different now. Adele is sleeping! NO coughing, NO wheezing, ALL sleeping. It is Tuesday morning and Janise and I are counting the days. Thursday evening is when our count down is at zero.

...from the bedside of The Lady Boss!

Andrew (Husband & Best Friend) 🖤

# May 29th

# Needs & Wants

Playlist
## Funkentelechy by Parliament

I always knew that our wants are in a constant state of change, moving towards the latest and greatest shiny object of the day. Satisfying our wants can lead us into temptation and deliver us to evil. I never thought about our needs and how they change based on our situation, and events in our lives.

**Needs & Wants!**
It was time to make a decision. Janise will not be driving in the near future, and we currently have two vehicles:

> 1. A Honda Pilot (a full size SUV family vehicle) which is more practical to transport Janise around town and Jabari to his baseball games; and
> 2. A Honda Civic Hatchback (6 speed manual transmission turbo sport touring).

> One vehicle has to GO!
> This morning I leave Janise at Providence, still rolling on my winter tires and rims. I head to pick up my summer rims and tires and have them placed into the back of my Honda Civic Hatchback (six speed manual transmission turbo sport touring) vehicle. Why not just put the damn tires on the car?

> Because it is our last day together.

> Being a grown-up and making responsible decisions sucks! I drive up to a Honda dealer in Brampton to hand back my Honda Civic Hatchback (six-speed manual transmission turbo sport touring) vehicle. On this last ride from Scarborough to Brampton the album of choice blasting through the speakers:

The 1977 album by Parliament - Funkentelechy vs. the Placebo Syndrome.

Track Listing of Funkentelechy vs the Placebo Syndrome by Parliament

**1. Bop Gun (Endangered Species)**
**2. Sir Nose D'Voidoffunk (Pay Attention-B3M)**
**3. Wizard Of Finance**
**4. Funkentelechy**
**5. Placebo Syndrome**
**6. Flash Light**

...from our Honda Pilot

Andrew (Husband & Best Friend) 🖤

# May 30<sup>th</sup>

## "Home"

Playlist
### Home by BJ The Chicago Kid

Janise insisted that her closet was to be packed in the morning. We have been counting the days down to this very day of May 30th; our count down is now at zero. She will be coming HOME in the evening. I pack Janise's clothes, various books, magazines, cards and plants. Janise is eager to help.

In the midst of our morning activities, we are visited by various nurse and therapy staff saying their tearful goodbyes. Our visits include favourite nurses, "Big Batty" Marcia and "The Beautiful" Rachel. We are provided with instructions on medicine, upcoming doctor visits, and outpatient speech and physiotherapy sessions to come. I return to Providence in the evening to bring Janise HOME.

We R HOME now and I am watching her sleep peacefully at 2am, May 31st. We had a great evening! Jabari welcomed his mom HOME, we ate some leftovers (chicken, brown rice and tomatoes), and watched the Raptor - Golden State game (Raptors WIN game one of the finals!)

We R HOME.

...from Our HOME

Andrew (Husband & Best Friend) ❤

# PART III

## Home at Last!

# June 1ˢᵗ

## Man's World?

Playlist
**It's A Man's World by James Brown**

This journey has been life changing for our family.

I have learned much about myself, Janise, our children, family, friends, and associates. I have seen the GOOD that we all have the capacity to achieve and particularly the GOOD that can be the byproduct of an illness. There have also been things that I have witnessed that I can't unsee; things I have heard that I can't unhear; and things I have felt, that I cannot unfeel. It ALL is part of the experience of life, something we can't change and shouldn't. ALL that we experience is responsible for the person we are today.

The GOOD, the bad, and the ugly.

I received various calls from Providence and Central East Community Care Access Centre (CCAC). Providence was reminding us of upcoming medical visits and CCAC was enquiring about how we were managing at home. CCAC now offers a "generous" one whole hour a day to help to bathe my wife and get her ready for the day. Ummm, let me see The Government bathing my wife. I took a pass on that one. Please leave some fun for me and my Teddy Pendergrass playlist! As long as I am physically able to do it, I-am-a-gonna-do-it!

I guess the next thing is to tag team the Government in to help me snuggle and spoon with Janise.

I did, however, take up the CCAC up on the home assessment service they offer and their assistance in making our HOME safe for Janise. I realize that I am definitely a MAN trapped in a MAN'S body!

This experience has me doing things that are truly unnatural to my nature. Like helping to put clothing on Janise. I have spent my life and perfected doing the exact opposite of this, it feels so WRONG! LOL!

Yesterday we took the time to plant the flowers and plants that Janise received from her many hospital visitors in our garden. Afterwards we will go for a nice long walk around our neighbourhood. Having Janise HOME is a blessing and something I will never take for granted again.

Playlist
**Ascension (Don't Ever Wonder) by Maxwell**

...from our HOME.

Andrew (Husband & Best Friend) ♥

# June 2nd

## Mighty & Brave

Saturday was a busy day!

We were up at 6:30am getting ready to go to Jabari's baseball game. There is no last minute anything in our lives now. Every movement, event, and occasion requires planning. There is no dividing up of life. No longer Janise managing task A, B, and C; and Andrew managing task D, E, and F. We do tasks A to F together.

I am not mad at that. When we divide up life, we do not spend time together. We are catching up on all that lost time over the years. The time was never wasted as it created, guided, and molded to of the best men I know—our sons Jelani and Jabari. The meaning of their names, you ask?

Jelani means MIGHTY; and Jabari means BRAVE.

MIGHTY is now 25-years-old and BRAVE is turning 17 in a couple of months. This would make Janise and I around the age of...you know—OLD! LOL! We watch BRAVE play baseball then host visitors at our home:

* My cousins visiting from New York, Noel and Tony;

* My mom;

* Janise's sister, Sharon, and her husband, Fewdel; and

* Janise's brother, Noel.

We joke, we laugh, we eat cake (courtesy of Sharon), drink tea and coffee, listen to old school reggae music, and pray for Janise. Tony leads a powerful prayer calling on God to heal and restore Janise 100 percent.

On the road to recovery Janise will remain an outpatient of Providence Healthcare attending speech therapy, occupational therapy, and physiotherapy sessions. Janise is physically strong but has balancing issues and memory issues. It is our hope and prayer that with the help of God she will be healed; please keep us in your prayers.

The goal now is to create a semblance of normalcy in our lives. It will not be the same old normal, but I promise you it will be:

A different normal;

A new normal;

A refreshing normal;

A better normal;

OUR normal.

Is this the vision of life that was expected? - No. Is it the perfect situation? - No. Can LOVE alone be strong enough to not only survive but thrive in this unexpected imperfect reality? - YES.

Playlist
## I'm Not Perfect (But I'm Perfect for You) by Grace Jones

...from our HOME .

Andrew (Husband & Best Friend).

# June 4<sup>th</sup>

## Familiarity

It is said that familiarity breeds contempt. Yet it is familiarity that provides us with our foundation, gives us comfort, and makes us feel safe. The music we LOVE, our family, friends, neighbours, and neighborhood. That grocery store, restaurant or watering hole we frequent, our gym, that television show, our home, and yes even our workplace. This familiarity is what makes you who you are.

We are more than the physical shell that we present to each other. Similar to an iceberg, much more of who we are is under the surface; in our case under our flesh and bones—unseen to the naked eye, hidden within our consciousness. Janise and I have been scoping out our neighbourhood, discovering each nook and cranny, all over again. Our adventures lead us to the neighborhood convenience store to pick up some items that we were running low on. Sunday would have us hosting family, my dad, Austin, and cousin, Monty. Our niece, Tanisha, and her son, with her parents, Sheda and Noel.

Their visits helped Janise's mind connect the dots of her relationship to each one of our visitors; the connection between the past and the present was evident in the BIG smile on Janise's face and her engaging conversations.

On Monday, Janise and I hung out all day at OUR office. She met clients/friends that she had not seen in many moons, once again her mind reconnecting the disconnections. Bringing past memories to the present.

Janise's healing is moving forward, a step at a time, a day at a time.

In our case FAMILIARITY breeds HEALING

...from our HOME.

Andrew (Husband & Best Friend) 💜

# June 4<sup>th</sup>

## "I'd Rather Be with You"

Playlist
### I'd Rather Be with You by Bootsy Collins

I am extremely lucky that my situation allows me the flexibility to work and take care of my wife at the same time. I am a self-employed accountant with an office in Scarborough offering professional tax, business advisory, and accounting services. I have been and will continue to take Janise to work with me as part of her therapy. She knows many of my clients and is happy to meet and interact with them. In turn, my clients are happy to meet and interact with Janise.

Kamay, a good friend and client for well over 25 years, popped by my office today. On his arrival Janise printed his name down on the paper she was writing on in front of her:

"K A M A Y".

This was exciting. Janise's eye hand coordination is coming back, her ability to write has returned through the connection of a true, blue friend from our past, present, and undoubtedly our future.

After several meetings with clients, Janise and I took a break and headed to a local Starbucks. We found a nice cozy two-seat table for our romantic mid-afternoon date. We shared egg bites, and a scone, and, of course, coffee.

Our date lasted a little over an hour. We picked this public place for our date, each of us with the ability to end it at any time. But that was not on the menu today; we seemed to have a connection with each other that went beyond the physical. There was an unknown, unlocked mystery about this lady across the table from me. I had the feeling that I had known this lady all my life yet was discovering her for the first time.

It was all so confusing!

I finally build up the nerve to cut through the superficial talk about the weather and the Toronto Raptors to get REAL. "Hey girl! I don't normally do this on a first date, but this is going so well," I say, and continue: "can I take you home with me for-the-rest-of-my-life?" LOL!

We return to the office to do work and head home at the end of the day. My bring-the-wife-to-work days have reinforced the fact that out of all the 7.5 billion people on this earth, I'd rather be with Janise!

...from our HOME.

Andrew (Husband & Best Friend). ♥

# June 6<sup>th</sup>

## Spring

We are in the midst of spring. Many of the signs of spring are present and accounted for:

* More sunlight
* Longer days
* The blooming of daffodils
* The leaves on the trees budding and growing
* Our scenery transitioning from gray to green
* Young LOVE and weddings
* Old LOVE and reminiscing
* The smell of spring
* The dogs & their dodo
* Rain, mud, cutting grass (repeat)
* The sighting of sports cars and motorcycles awakening from their long winter hibernation
* No sightings of the Toronto Maple Leafs playing hockey in the Stanley Cup finals
* Lots of promises that next season will be better for the Toronto Maple Leafs

That damn bird has once again out-strategized me; there is a fully functioning bird's nest taking shelter in the ceiling area of the porch of our home. Like the "glorious" Maple Leafs, I make many promises that next year I will do better and outsmart that bird! My home will not be the bird's home any longer! This is the last year!

In the theme of spring, we have been doing an overall cleaning and clearing up. From removing rugs from the flooring of our home to avoid Janise slipping and falling, to clearing closets and drawers of all the human dodo we seem to have in abundance.

Yesterday, in between work, Janise and I visited a local Service Ontario to update my old red and white Ontario Health Card with an updated picture health card. The old red and white card is no longer accepted for our free health care in Canada. So, I now have replaced it with the new picture health care card. (Yes, Americans, we have free health care paid via of everyone's taxes. The concept is simple: everyone helps everyone.)

In the late afternoon, we visit my mom who re-braids Janise's hair and, as mothers do, feeds us a belly full of delicious food. At the end of the day, we are HOME, watching the game three victory of the Toronto Raptors over the Golden State Warriors!

I hope the Toronto Maple Leafs take time out of their vacation to watch the Raptors' win.

...from our HOME

Andrew (Husband & Best Friend) ♥

# June 6ᵗʰ

## Memories

The events of our lives can all be sectioned off and stored within our mind in logical segments of time: days, weeks, months, and years. When our brain has been interrupted by an injury (in the case of Janise, a stroke) there can be an impact to accessing those logical segments of time stored meticulously within our mind. Janise was in Scarborough General and Providence Health Care hospitals for a combined 73 days (March 18th to May 30th). Janise missed out on the later part of March and the months of April and May in the battle to BE.

If the task at hand was to simply update Janise on the two-and-a-half months she missed of the outside world that would be child's play. In some cases, Janise's memories exist, but the timeline has been damaged. In some other cases her memories are damaged, or they may exist but access to them have been damaged. In either case it leads to very interesting, frustrating, amusing, emotional, comical, and ALWAYS LOVING conversations.

Jabari, Jelani and I possess the patience of Job (the biblical figure that demonstrated an unyielding degree of patience, faith, and conviction despite the difficulties he faced). We work LOVINGLY with Janise to help her work through the fog and confusion she experiences. We never miss an opportunity to introduce a joke or tease Janise whenever humanly possible. Trust me she hits us back with jokes and teasing just as hard.

This is our way! This is how we deal with adversity. This is how Janise will HEAL. Laughter is the greatest medicine of all.

Playlist
### Remember the Time by Michael Jackson

...from our HOME.

Andrew (Husband & Best Friend)

# June 9<sup>th</sup>

## "...& God Created Woman"

There is such wisdom in the architecture and the creation of the universe, our planet, nature, WOMAN, and MAN. In particular, the interdependence and interconnectedness amongst us and between us, which also extends to our surroundings: nature, the earth and the greater universe.

For obvious reasons, I have been in tune with the interdependent and interconnected relationship between MAN and WOMAN; this is at the forefront of each day of my life now.

...& GOD Created Woman

GOD (otherwise known as Jehovah, Allah, Yahweh, The Father, Elohim, El-Shaddai, Abba, Jah; and for the members of the Beehive, Beyonce, LOL!) showed true wisdom in the creation of MAN & WOMAN. We each have characteristics that add to each other. When we get together the sum of what each of us brings to the relationship is actually far greater than each of us individually. Where MAN fails WOMAN succeeds and vice versa.

There is wisdom in WOMEN being in possession of the "vessel of life," in WOMEN sayin' NO (so damn often), in WOMEN knowing their worth. In MAN having to step up their game, in MAN earning the LOVE of their Queen.

Perhaps I am a dinosaur with ancient thoughts and ways for this new world; but these ancient ways are also my ways. They are the ideals not necessarily the reality that is always achieved, but what are we if we are not reaching for these ideals?

The superpower of my WOMAN has always been her POWERFUL mind. She memorized everyone's phone number, everyone's schedules, every GOOD, bad and ugly thing from my past, and as a result NEVER lost an argument.

Now KRYPTONITE, in the form of a stroke, has been introduced into our lives and has impacted her SUPERPOWER. We now battle together against this common enemy in order to restore Janise back to her former self. Foolishly, I long for the days to be mentally tripped up by Janise and once again go back to the comfort of losing arguments.

I also look forward to being reminded of what we were both wearing when I asked her to marry me, and other key details of our 37-year relationship. Unfortunately, I outsourced all the beautiful details to Janise's beautiful mind, so it needs to get BETTER.

For now, wifey & I roll together as ONE, at work rest and play. I am now the keeper of the memories of the beautiful details of OUR LIFE & LOVE .

Playlist
## Remember the Time by Michael Jackson

...from OUR HOME.

Andrew (Husband & Best Friend).

# June 12<sup>th</sup>

## Advocacy

Advocacy can be defined as speaking on behalf of, standing up for, and supporting another person. A pure and true act of compassion, looking out for the well-being of another soul. With life comes a lot of noise and distractions. Sifting through this murky cloud is tough enough for yourself, this becomes even more intense when you are doing this 4-the-One-U-LOVE.

Janise's illness has given us both the opportunity to slow life down, and the space to reflect.

The process has been cathartic. The time we previously filled with chasing our tails is now replaced with thoughtful analysis, planning, and purposeful action. Our thoughtful analysis has extended beyond Janise's medical situation to work, rest and play; otherwise known as OUR lives. Time for you to plan.

**Consider:**

* Who is looking out for you?
* Who is looking for you to succeed?
* Who has your best interest in mind?
* Who has got your back?
* Who will BE with YOU when the going gets tough?
* Who is simply "mailing it in"?
* Who is your RIDE or DIE?

These tough questions are asked with NO apologies!

Playlist
### Rebel Without a Pause by Public Enemy

Riding shotgun with Janise.

...from OUR HOME.

Andrew (Husband & Best Friend).

# June 12<sup>th</sup>

## Irie

**IRIE** [ ay-ri ]

*Noun*

Nice, pleasant, good vibrations

The morning started out irie! We dropped Jabari off at school, and Janise and I headed to the office to meet clients and get work done.

Everything was irie!

Balance.

Playlist
### Irie Ites by Third World

Overall, since Janise has come home from the hospital, we have achieved a good balance in our life between work life and home life. Janise has been improving in terms of memory and mobility however still struggles with her balance. Sometimes she appears to have everything together in terms of standing, sitting, and walking.

The stairs are a challenge, Janise requires assistance maneuvering up and down stairs. I imagine that running, the triple jump, high jump, and the pole vault may also prove to be difficult for Janise, but I do not have a definitive answer on this at this point in time.

Towards the end of the day, Janise had a fall. I was there but late on reacting. I was able to grab her before she hit the ground and raise her to standing; however she did hit her side against a small table in my office.

Janise with chest pains!

My guilt! Then the rush to Scarborough General Hospital emergency!

- X-rays.
- 2 broken ribs!
- Extra strength Tylenol pain medication recommendation.

My guilt is now tenfold!

Janise is and will be fine; ribs apparently heal themselves. There will be pain management for the next couple of weeks, however, there are no signs or symptoms of stroke.

I get it. Janise now gets it: It takes time to get to the right balance. So my girl has a few more wounds, and more stories from the battlefield. These wounds will heal and help to build a stronger (and even more stubborn) Janise.

The day has ended and returned once again to the irie vibes of the morning. I joke with Janise, letting her know that her trade-in value will continue to diminish if she keeps getting hurt LOL! Coincidentally, the meat I seasoned to cook for dinner was ribs. Having brown rice, green salad, tomatoes, and avocados with it.

Should I be worried that I took out chicken legs to thaw, season, and cook for tomorrow? Perhaps Janise should not leave our bed tomorrow!

...from OUR HOME.

Andrew (Husband & Best Friend) 🖤

# June 15<sup>th</sup>

## "Unconditional"

It has been a week of high highs and low lows. I have seen it ALL this week.

**LOW LOWS**

- Janise's fall.
- The fracturing of 2 of Janise's ribs.
- The pain Janise is dealing with as a result of her injury.

**HIGH HIGHS**

After a full check up at the hospital, Janise is GOOD, with the exception of her ribs. Ribs heal themselves. Jabari and Jelani's LOVE and support for their Mom.

- Spending every hour of time with my best friend.
- My UNCONDITIONAL LOVE  for Janise.
- Becoming reacquainted and reconnected with Janise in the REAL world outside the confines of an institution.
- The support of my brother-in-law Noel Campbell whose assistance with Janise and help with preparing OUR HOME for Janise's arrival, (renovations and painting) has been invaluable!

Observing the LOVE, compassion and helpful words and helping hands of family and friends. Eye-C-U-ALL! The support of:

* My Parents
* My Brother's (Mike and Eddie Mac) and their families
* Janise's mother and sisters
* Cousins, aunts, uncles, and nieces and nephews all over the world (Caribbean, Africa, Europe, and North America)
* Friends and colleagues

Playlist
## Unconditional by Jacksoul

...from OUR HOME.

Andrew (Husband & Best Friend) ♥

# June 16<sup>th</sup>

## Kitchener

Yesterday Janise and I were in the city of Kitchener watching Jabari's baseball team the Stouffville Yankees play a double header baseball game against the Kitchener Panthers. In addition, I put in a formal written complaint to Mother Nature's ombudsman. It was June 15th and the sun was playing hooky for the day.

Perhaps it is staying in Oakland, California celebrating the amazing NBA championship win of the Toronto Raptors over the Golden State Warriors in the home of the Warriors, Oracle Arena. RAPTORS RULE!.

The day was cold, although the app on my phone proclaimed a temperature of 17 Celsius, "the devil is a liar". We were wrapped in blankets to keep warm and protected from the brisk and unforgiving wind; covered under a massive golf umbrella to stay dry. We do all of this for the proud opportunity to see our child shine in the game he loves, that's what parents do!

**We warmed from this experience:**

* Watching Jabari play;
* From the camaraderie of sharing the pain of the inclement weather with the other baseball parents; and
* By drinking HOT CHOCOLATE.

Coincidentally HOT CHOCOLATE, and BIG DADDY are a couple of my nicknames; don't worry Janise these salacious stories will travel with me to my grave LOL!

We warmed also from reconnecting with various players and parents from the Kitchener Panthers team. We all travelled to Cuba a couple of years ago as the Canadian contingent to play against various Cuban baseball teams. Janise remembered the parents and players from the Cuba trip, and we reminisced about old times.

Playlist
**They Reminisce Over You (T.R.O.Y.) (Flashback)
by Pete Rock, CL Smooth**

The day became warm and sunny not externally but internally. I understood the purpose and withdrew my complaint to Mother Nature's ombudsman.

...from OUR HOME

Happy Father's Day to all the Big Daddys!

Andrew (Husband, Best Friend, Father, "HOT CHOCOLATE" and "BIG DADDY" LOL!). ♥

# June 18<sup>th</sup>

## "We Are One"

*In Kitchener Ontario at Jabari's baseball game*

There has been a reinvention of the roles Janise and I play within our relationship with each other, our children, family, friends and colleagues.

This reinvention has fortified our commitment to each other through a rekindling of our relationship.

Everything GOOD, comfortable, and familiar remains; yet we have discovered a hidden next level and with it a newness, a oneness, a wholeness. Like back in the day when you accidentally discovered that hidden bonus level while playing Nintendo's Super Mario Brothers! Yes! That same feeling can be experienced outside of a video game! I know crazy right!?

Playlist
**We Are One by Ziggy Marley**

I have also felt a oneness with family and friends who have graciously shared their experiences with their illness, and the illness of their Loved Ones; I have been taking notes and learning.

Janise remains on the road to recovery. Being in the familiar setting of HOME has had a dramatic positive impact on her wellbeing. She is slowly recovering her short-term memory, and sorting, organizing, and making sense of the vast library of her long-term memory.

I, of course, have been assisting in this process adding certain "Easter eggs" in Janise's mind with the goal of creating a 2019 version of my own little Stepford Wife (insert evil diabolical laugh here ).

Yesterday was about family, connecting with good friends and of course The Toronto Raptors NBA Championship victory parade in Toronto.

Yesterday, the city, province, and nation became ONE.

...from OUR HOME.

Andrew (Husband, Best Friend & Bandwagon Toronto Raptors  Fan) ❤

# June 19<sup>th</sup>

## Just the Facts

In between work, our days are filled with various medical thangs!

Ensuring the connections are connected on the 28-day Holter Janise is strapped to, baby aspirin to prevent Janise's blood from clotting, extra strength Tylenol for her fractured ribs, medical appointments, and therapy appointments.

Fun fact: The word "Blood Clot" is actually a curse word in Jamaica! Now I know why.

It was time to change it up!

Do some"thang" completely different!

We are going to make our own little video!

But Andrew you say:

That kind of raunchy stuff is for the foolish kids who are in love.

What about the internet if it leaks?

You can't undo this!

Ain't nobody want to see Dat! Especially at your age!

Get your minds out of the gutter! SHAME! HONESTLY! Janise & I.....Ok at least Janise is a respectable member of this society.

Seriously though the idea came from my sister-in-law, we were talking about the movie *50 First Dates*. In this movie Drew Barrymore suffers from short-term memory loss, to keep her up to date on her current life, Adam Sandler who plays her boyfriend records a video she watches everyday.

It is a GREAT Idea, and I completed the video on my cell phone.

Fun Fact: It is rumored that cell phones were once used to make phone calls, but I don't believe it #fakenews

So, the video is complete, and Janise is reminded everyday as she watches it:

* She had a stroke on March 18th which put her in a coma for several days;
* She was hospitalized for 2.5 months;
* Her ribs are sore from a fall, and two of her ribs are fractured;
* The current year;
* The birthdate and ages of Jabari, Jelani, her and I;
* She lives to satisfy and service her husband who was in 2019 voted The Sexist Man Alive.

Reminding her of these "FACTS", has made the world of difference in her recovery LOL!

...from OUR HOME.

Andrew (Husband, Best Friend & 2019's SEXIEST MAN ALIVE). ❤

# June 20<sup>th</sup>

## Questions

Life often offers more questions than answers. We have no answers as to why Janise had a stroke, nothing but questions.

* Our family has questions;
* Our friends and colleagues have questions; and
* Those who work in the medical system have questions.

No one has answers!

At the end of the day there are things in this life that are within our control and things in this life that are beyond our control.

One of the things within our control; the things we put in our mouths.

I am head of groceries and cooking duties in our home and hence responsible for everything that my wife puts in her mouth.

EVERYTHING!

This is a BIG responsibility.

Improving our eating habits, eating as healthy as possible has got to be at least part of the answer.

So, I have been studying and researching ways of eating:

* Keto;
* Paleo;
* Vegetarian;
* One Meal A Day;

...and the search continues.

In the meantime, and in-between time, I have rested on a lifestyle for Janise and I of zero carbs for six days and one cheat day where carbs are permitted--but good carbs (sweet potatoes, yams, and brown rice).

And vegetarian? Damn it! I got a Big Green Egg Smoker BBQ that downright demands beef, chicken, and fish. But goodbye bread, goodbye duck bread, goodbye white rice, goodbye pizza, goodbye bun and cheese. Know that it's not you CARBS--it's ME. US.

"Parting is such sweet sorrow, That I shall say good night till it be morrow."
*Romeo & Juliet* by Shakespeare.

...from OUR HOME.

Andrew (Husband, Best Friend, & CARB FREE) . 🖤

# June 23$^{rd}$

## Road Trip

Who doesn't LOVE a good old fashion weekend road trip?

Playlist
### Fast Car by Tracy Chapman

Eh? Huh? Well…

Like the:

Packing of way too many clothes; enough clothing to last us at least one week yet the trip is only for two nights and three days.

Mad rush to get everything done at home, work for the clients, and in this case the last final exam before the summer break for Jabari.

Loading up the Honda Pilot with luggage, the cooler, portable chairs, umbrellas, Jabari's baseball gear, and—oh yes—the trip participants Jabari, Janise, and I.

Let's GO!

Then the rush to hurry up only to get stopped, stalled, and frustrated by GTA traffic from Toronto to Hamilton. As despite all the planning and strategy undoubtedly, we finally get rolling just in time to catch rush hour….

 %@#$!

Most important though is we are on our way: the journey has begun.

Music is played, there is singing, a movie is put in for Jabari to watch in the back and listen through his headphones; every time we pass a farm I am accused of farting in the car by my "LOVING " family (…maybe it is time to check out my digestive system!).

The destination, The "B'Lo", Buffalo, New York. Home of the Bills, Sabres, and the Bisons (The Toronto Blue Jays farm team).

We are safely within the Canadian Health Care System for Janise while being two and a half hours—a stones throw—away from the Canadian border. We are headed to the land known as America aka The USA, aka 'Merica! It is literally another country, another land, with different ways, strange customs. They say **YES** to guns and **NO** to education and health care...to each their own.

The experience has been GREAT!

The hotel, the baseball. OUR family, our baseball family, Buffalo chicken wings, and salad (sayin' **NO** to carbs).

Gots-to-GO. Early game on Sunday. Time to sleep.

...from the "B'Lo".

Andrew (Husband, Best Friend &...maybe I will actually check out my digestive system). ♥

# June 25<sup>th</sup>

## Helping vs. Independence

Helping and assisting can actually have the exact opposite result than anticipated. Your help can lead to the detriment of a situation.

We attended an outpatient physio assessment and speech therapy session yesterday at Providence Health Care Centre where this nugget of information was revealed.

Every morning I am hands on (both of my hands) in showering and dressing Janise. I must be honest my efforts are not necessarily for Janise's benefit alone—if ya know what I'm sayin'. But there is an aspect of doin' for the ONE U LOVE, not just doin' the ONE U LOVE LOL!

The purpose of rehabilitation though is independence. Janise must become an Independent WOMAN and build to do for herself. And cue song...

Playlist
### Independent Women by Destiny's Child

(This song selection was specifically for our niece, the #1 Beyonce fan in the world! Respect the Beehive)

The physio and speech session also provided us with two additional tools to help Janise with her memory that we have put into practice.

1  A daily journal summarizing the activities of the day in a calendar book.

2  A chalk board on an easel in the living room where Janise writes the current date every day and key upcoming activities.

The Rehab Team LOVED the idea of the five minute video I show to Janise everyday (a BIG THANK YOU to my sister-in-law Sharon Jones for this GREAT IDEA) to update her on the fact that:

✓ She had a stroke;

✓ Her rib injury;

✓ The year;

✓ Family birthdays and ages; and her life goal to service and please me (and the Beehive says).

...I may have skipped over the last point in my explanation of the video with the Rehab Team, but the point is they LOVED the concept.

...from OUR HOME.

Andrew (Husband & Best Friend). 🖤

# June 26<sup>th</sup>

## The View U Have of U

Playlist

### How Do Yeaw View You? by Funkadelic

The most important view of you is the view you have of you (repeat).

The need to impress others and be loved by many is actually not a need at all but a foolish want. This particular want leads many into an endless loop of wasted time and effort.

At this time in our lives Janise and I are happy to BE.

Happy to BE:

- ✓ together;
- ✓ In LOVE with ourselves;
- ✓ In LOVE with each other;
- ✓ Surrounded by LOVE;
- ✓ Stronger together, than we are individually;
- ✓ More than what is expected;
- ✓ Defiant in our unyielding demands for a better life;
- ✓ Unphased by the attempts to limit OUR path and potential; and
- ✓ Unaffected by the naysayers.

We are fully committed to OUR LIFE it's blessings, and its challenges.

Every day brings us more and more tools to assist in the recovery of Janise. We utilize pictures, videos, daily journals, a chalk board, mind and body exercises, singing, music, and dancing all to get Janise back to JANISE!

OUR investment in this project: the precious, valuable, limited, and shrinking resource that we hold so dear in our later years—TIME.

Playlist
## Time by The Last Poets

...from OUR HOME.

Andrew (Husband & Best Friend). ♥

# June 26<sup>th</sup>

## "Joy in Repetition"

Playlist
**Joy in Repetition by Prince**

A large part of our daily life is repetitive, lacking in variety. Some would classify this aspect of life as being dull, boring, and monotonous. But our perspective can change based on our viewing angle. When we are able to understand the purpose of our daily tasks and rituals, we can see them in a different light, it can be like switching from viewing a black and white television to viewing a 4K television—yes, that dramatic!

> Our daily rituals have purpose.
> Waking up in the morning—Thank you, God, for yet another day on Earth!
> There is joy in repetition!
> Eating healthy to promote and extend life.
> There is joy in repetition!
> Daily mind and body exercises to rebuild, restore, and re-create Janise.
> There is joy in repetition!
> Spending time together at work, rest, and play—to grow and expand the
> LOVE-for-one-another
> There is joy in repetition!

> Being surrounded by the circle of LOVE from family, friends, colleagues and the wider community - To reap the benefits of the seeds that we have sown throughout our lives.
> There is joy in repetition!

> Holding, supporting & LOVING Janise—to let her know that I am with her with each step, slip, and fall. Every time she rises up to repeat this scenario and when she no longer repeats this scenario.

Yes, there is joy is repetition!

JOY

...from Our HOME.

Andrew (Husband & Best Friend) 🖤

# July 1ˢᵗ

## It's the Weekend Baby!

*Janise showing off her nails done by our friend Carol Roberts*

We fit a lot into this holiday weekend: a BBQ, home renovations, visits from friends & family, pedicure and manicure, dancing & singing. Whew!

Thank GOD Monday is a holiday; this brother needs to rest!

**Saturday**

After visits from my niece and her family we attended a family BBQ. It was nice to be out on a non-medical excursion and enjoy good company, food, drinks & laughs. Everyone was happy and excited seeing Janise out and about, and vertical. Many of the BBQ attendees last saw Janise horizontal in a hospital bed.

Fun Fact: I still have the pleasure of seeing Janise horizontal in OUR bed at HOME...If ya know what I'm sayin'.

## Sunday

My brother-in-law, Noel, and I continued our mission from GOD to complete the renovations. Admittedly, like all home improvements, this one was hit with what industry experts call scope creep, but this is par for the course.

I was dressed in my painting clothes taking orders from Noel: "paint this wall, ceiling, door and base board," while he worked on the kitchen backsplash. Meanwhile we had many visitors keeping Janise company.

They brought delicious foods and snacks. One friend ended up using his talents to help Noel out with the kitchen backsplash, the music was blasting while Janise enjoyed girl time with friends who gave Janise a much-needed manicure and pedicure.

Fun Fact: Despite the tremendous help and support that I have received from ALL of the men in my life during these trying times, I would NOT touch the FEET of any of these DUDES unless a loaded gun was pointed at my temple. And even then, there would be a thought process:

"Andrew, you have lived a good life. Is touching this dude's feet worth extending it?".

Later in the day the music continued to blast, some guests left, and other family arrived while Noel and I continued our mission from GOD. Then an impromptu dance party broke out!

Our part-time chef and nail specialist had put on her DJ "Selecta" hat, busting out tunes from YouTube that had everyone dancing and singing, with Janise leading the way!

The day was full, fun and productive. Renovations should be more or less completed by Monday, our bellies were full, Janise's nails were on point, we got great exercise, and most of all we all shared TIME and LOVE.

...from OUR HOME

Andrew (Husband & Best Friend) 🖤

# July 3<sup>rd</sup>

## Who Are You?

The inner essence of who we are is revealed in times of stress, anger, sickness and my favourite inebriation. In my book blaming bad behaviour on the situation or alcohol just doesn't cut it.

During these times the protective walls that we have taken our lifetimes to mason become transparent or even crumble, revealing our authentic selves.

For some this authenticity can be rather disturbing and will lead those who witness it to cry out:

"Build that wall!".

But alas, as we have learned Mexico ain't gonna pay to rebuild this or any other imaginary wall.

Before Janise's sickness she was the light in a dark room, possessing the power and strength and disruptive energy of a hurricane. People were attracted to her positive spirit and the noise that surrounded her.

She was never one to take time outs, sit still or do one thing at a time. You marvelled witnessing how she moved through life.

In sickness Janise tires easily performing physical activities, requires more rest than I have ever seen her take, and is quiet.

Yet she continues to BE the attraction of our attention through her now calm, peaceful nature. She remains positive and LOVING; the REAL Janise!

Her caring nature is front and centre; even at this time she places the needs of others before her very own.

It is very strange times indeed, when I as a man am asking my wife to speak louder, and to engage in conversation.

"Tell me about what your thinking and feeling; hun?"

Am I in a Twilight Zone episode?!

Perhaps we are within the eye of the storm called Janise, where all is quiet before we are once again within the heat of the storm.

Perhaps this is the new Janise.

Perhaps we will end up somewhere in between these extremes.

Wherever we end up it will BE the Janise I will continue 2 LOVE and support.

Playlist
## Come as You Are by Nirvana

...from OUR HOME.

Andrew (Husband & Best Friend).

**PART IV**

*New Normal*

# July 5th

## Going Down

Playlist
**Paid in Full by Eric B. and Rakim**

Janise and I are on six days of protein and vegetables with one cheat day where carbohydrates are allowed. All to improve our health by changing what we put in our mouths.

I am happy to also report that we are both going DOWN and it feels GREAT!

* Amazing!

* Energizing!

* Exuberating!

* Orgasmic!

As those of you who like myself are PURE of heart realize, I am obviously referring to going down in weight!

We are both down by about eight pounds since we have changed what we eat.
The protein we have been eating a lot lately is fish ("which is my favourite dish"); and of course boiled eggs every day for breakfast. Chicken and pork are also on heavy rotation in our meal plan.

In terms of vegetables, we are loving asparagus, cabbage, broccoli, cauliflower, and the traditional salad which join the protein on our plates.

We have become very creative with our meals using a combination of our Smith and Campbell family recipes and YouTube.

Opting to use the real "thang" in terms of cutting up garlic, onions, green peppers, and green onions over the powdered forms of these same seasonings. And we're keeping the salt intake at a minimum.

Going DOWN requires dedication, creativity and patience. Going DOWN has never felt so good...as a reminder the topic of discussion is weight; LOL!

...from OUR HOME.

Andrew (Husband and Best Friend).

# July 7ᵗʰ

## Your Garden

Playlist
### Potholes in my Lawn by De La Soul

Gardening has always been a hobby that I have thoroughly enjoyed as it mirrors our very existence on this earth.

The seed sprouts New Life in the spring, there is a period of growth and strength, the growing season.

Then there is a time of preparedness; preparing to go back to the soil from which was the very source of life.

With the inevitable approach of Autumn and Winter comes the end of the life span of the plant or flower.

This cycle then repeats come Spring.

The garden has all of the basic fundamentals required for life, but life but does require assistance from above in the form of rain and sun for life to BE.

We are no different.

In addition, we must de-weed our gardens. Clearing out the disruptive life forms and allowing the population of the garden to reach their life potential. This also has the by-product of revealing the true beauty of each life within the garden and the garden itself.

We are no different.

Janise and I did some gardening yesterday! Actually, I did the grunt work under Janise's supervision and instruction:

* Pulling weeds;

* Trimming trees, plants and bushes;

* Bagging the weeds for city pick up; and

* Sweeping up and cleaning up.

Janise however did swoop in to take over the duties of watering the garden.

With this overdue task complete and clarity achieved, we spent the afternoon barbecuing, eating, drinking, playing music, singing and dancing with family and friends.

On this day reaching our life's potential by sharing our most valued commodity with others; TIME.

...from OUR HOME.

Andrew (Husband & Best Friend). 🖤

# July 9<sup>th</sup>

## Our Brain

Neuroplasticity allows our brain to rewire functions from areas that have been damaged to new and healthy parts of the brain.

To trigger this, repetition is key. Whatever we do over and over again we become better at ...

(insert lovemaking joke right about HERE!, and pause to enjoy your AMAZING joke; let it breathe).

It has become evident that Jabari, Jelani and my history of being jokers is a bit of a double edge sword.

Although humour does work to lighten things up and is a great mechanism to deal with stress, it works against you when trying to convince your loved one of certain facts, current events, and known realities.

In particular, Janise seems to need corroborating evidence for near everything that comes out of my mouth. Just yesterday she phoned my Mom to confirm some information I was telling her.! She only believed my information when confirmed by my Mom!

Well, I guess this is actually things as they always have been, given my history of trying to trick and fool Janise through my many pranks.

This part of her brain and memories seems to be working overtime.

"Yes, Hun the people actually elected that guy!; Really!"

"No Janise, you are not 35 years old (from your mouth to God's ears though!)."

"Jabari will be 17 years old in August and Jelani is 25 years old."

"Bill Cosby is now known for serving people stronger stuff than Jello Pudding."

"Oh yea, this IS a NEW Law. All wives are now required to do this for their husbands.

Please let's NOT break this law!"

We continue in Janise's recovery using journals, videos, pictures, gatherings, walking, therapy, medical appointments and tests, talking, spending time together and loving each other.

Our task is to assist in this brain rewiring exercise...

Let's see: red wire, black wire, white wire; —now where did I see the ground wire?

...from OUR HOME.

Andrew (Husband & Best Friend). 🖤

# July 11<sup>th</sup>

## Golden Shower

This week included a doctor's visit, a hairdressing and nail appointment, and a cooking session with a true friend.

### Doctor Visit

Janise is under constant medical supervision. This week we had an appointment with our family doctor for a general check up. All went well.

We were then sent to the lab for blood work. As is common with me, the initial lady taking the blood work had a bit of trouble finding Janise's vein, however her supervisor took over and made quick work of extracting the blood sample.

They then handed us a container the size of a pill bottle and asked Janise to collect a sample of her urine in it!

Janise is not yet stable on her feet. I then would have to witness the event in the lady's washroom and not get arrested.

A task I was willing and a little excited to take on!

This would be my R. Kelly moment.

Let's just say that us men can learn from the pinpoint aim of the opposite sex! Impressive!

### "Hair Did!"

Yesterday Janise had a hair appointment with Paula and a nail appointment with Nikki of www.nikandpea.com.

Jabari also had his hair twisted ala Snoop Dogg. The D, O, double G representing the LBC (Long Beach, California crew). Jabari is representing SCARBOROUGH.

We all had great conversation about sports, music and life in general!

**Cooking Session**

Tracey Brissett Grose Our friend, joined us at the salon and later at home to cook a delicious dinner with the assistance of Janise. The dinner consisted of ribs, stir fry vegetables, and a mango salad.

Later, we all walked off the dinner with our now traditional late night neighborhood stroll.

It has been a GOOD week with even BETTER days to come.

...from OUR HOME.

Andrew (Husband & Best Friend).

# July 12<sup>th</sup>

## Speechless

Thank You.

Playlist
### Thank You by Sly and the Family Stone

There are a few small words when combined together have a tremendous impact on those on the receiving end of these words.

The impact is GREAT because these words are combined with purpose and meaning, and very often related to an event, situation and/or a relationship with its shared trials, tribulations, failures, and successes.

"I Love You";

"God Bless You"; and

"Thank You".

The strange thing is that we are on the receiving end of these beautiful words when we are simply doing what is RIGHT, what we are SUPPOSED to do.

We must then shed our discomfort when these words are thrown to us and simply accept them; they are very heavy words, never to be used or accepted in a nonchalant manner.

Despite being within the trees and having a bird's eye view of the forest and the journey, the effort and dedication to navigate it's untouched trails has never been lost on me. However, to be recognized and appreciated for this beautiful struggle from:

* friends;

family; and

most of all, from my beautiful wife (to whom I am only doing for her as she would do for me). leaves me, miraculously, without words...

...from OUR HOME.

Andrew (Husband & Best Friend).

# July 15<sup>th</sup>

## Toronto Beach

*Our Toronto Beach Selfie*

* Sun

* Boardwalk

* Sand

* Water & , most of all

* LOVE

- Toronto Beaches July 2019.


Playlist

**On Your Face by Earth Wind & Fire**

...from The Beaches.


Andrew (Husband & Best Friend).

# July 17<sup>th</sup>

## Words

Playlist
### Wordy Rappinghood by Tom Tom Club

I learned that talking is good exercise for the brain as it helps the brain arrange and align information, and in the case of Janise rearrange and realign information.

This gives me a whole new insight into the opposite sex; women do not talk a lot they are simply constantly arranging and aligning information in their brains.

Interesting.

While I have always verbalized the thoughts and feelings of my inner voice out LOUD!, I am using so many WORDS that my inner voice has now taken over my outer voice...they are ONE.

All to evoke communication, conversation, discussion, laughter even discourse. Whatever it takes, whatever it calls for to inspire verbal communication with Janise.

* We talk while we get ready for the day
* We talk while we eat meals
* We talk while we work
* We talk while we are at home
* We talk while we walk the neighbourhood
* We talk while we go to bed
* We talk while we...

I think I better stop here before I share too much!

WORDS have never been more meaningful. So, I now fill our previously comfortable silent moments with:; WORDS.

- Need water!
- Mouth dry!

...from OUR HOME.

Andrew (Husband & Best Friend).

# July 18<sup>th</sup>

## Man vs. Prostate Exam

An occupational therapist visits our home on Tuesdays and Thursdays for one hour each time. Janise did well at her occupational therapy session today; showing vast improvement in both her eye- hand coordination and her balance.

Now it was my turn to go to the doctor for a checkup after more than 10 years!

Janise's recent illness made everything REAL!

I am a man who is over 50 years old!

There is a long list of medical stuff to watch for after being on this earth over half a century. The good news is my weight, blood pressure, heart rate, and other vitals are on point.

It is however amazing that we can send a man to the moon, build a self-driving electric car, have voice activated phones, electronics and even homes; yet to check a man's prostate we are back in 1812!

Really this is how we check the prostate?!

Isn't there an app to check a man's prostate?

No?

Then there should be!

#me2

Seriously though, I do strongly advise everyone to go get themselves checked out; if not for yourself, then at least for your loved ones.

To all the men out there: it is also advisable to examine the size of your doctor's hands before committing to a check up ... just sayin' .

...from OUR HOME.

Andrew (Husband & Best Friend).

# July 25<sup>th</sup>

## Happy Anniversary

### June 1982

- Connection
- Friendship
- Love
- Commitment
- Devotion

### July 25, 1992

- Marriage
- Public expression of love and & Commitment

### April 21, 1994

- Love is a verb – Jelani

### August 17, 2002

- I said Love is a verb – Jabari

### July 25, 2019

- Our 27th Wedding Anniversary & our 37th year in our relationship
- We celebrate our boys; view these products of our love with awe
-Reflect on our beautiful life together
- Cook a delicious meal of roasted chicken, roasted asparagus, and a very colourful salad
- After dinner we cheat off of our meal plan, sneaking off away for a fudge sundae (My family and I will pay for this slip in judgement. Me via my lactose intolerance, and my family by witnessing my body rejecting the fudge sundae)
We continue the movement forward with the theme to live, laugh, and Love.

It's our anniversary!

Playlist
## Anniversary by Tony! Toni! Toné!

...from OUR HOME.

Andrew (Husband & Best Friend).

# August 5<sup>th</sup>

## Were Only Human

We are human.

This condition has made us the walking contradictions we see before us. We are magnificent yet insignificant, powerful yet weak, perfect yet flawed.

We often project our own perspectives onto everyone's timeline. Proclaiming with great reverence and conviction whether a given day was GOOD or BAD. Yet the day was no different from any other day; the sun rises in the east and sets in the west.

We may not be in control of all what happens within our days, but we are in control of our own interpretations of our experiences.

Janise is now working through her life story. Her long-term memory is inconsistent. Some existing without a reference point or logical timeline. Her short-term memory is at best spotty. We are all playing the role of putting the various pieces of her memories / life story back together with her. Janise is improving over time; we do, however, know that we are running a marathon and not a sprint.

This has been a beautiful, frustrating, happy, somber, glorious, unpleasant, and LOVING experience.

An experience that mirrors the human condition. An experience that I am happy to repeat, as the goal is PURE.

...from OUR HOME.

Andrew (Husband & Best Friend). 🖤

# August 9<sup>th</sup>

## Overflowing Cup

Janise is a Libra and true to her zodiac sign has been a proponent of balance and fairness. Relationships are important to Janise as she is concerned mainly with the happiness of the people in her life maneuvers through social situations effortlessly with her charming personality.

Fun Fact: My zodiac sign is Aries which is actually the opposite sign of Libra; Aries symbolizing the "ME", Libra symbolizing the "WE".

### Strength

Physically strong, pre-stroke in the gym, Janise could back squat well over her weight. .

Mentally strong, once Janise sets her mind to a task, it gets done; and she does what she wants to do!

Who is Janise? Janise is:

- Balance and fairness;
- Passionate about justice;
- Charming;
- intelligent;
- Physically strong; and
- Mentally strong.

All GREAT characteristics to have to survive, recover and thrive after a stroke.

Beautiful

Not so GREAT characteristics when we have to get to an appointment and Janise decides "I ain't going nowhere! I am staying at home today!"

Arrrgh! Yet I secretly take pride in her defiance of my fledgling command and control over her comings and goings.

I welcome back the woman I married as she storms back up the stairs to our home, refusing to go anywhere with me on this day.

Playlist
## Here I Come by Dennis Brown

...from OUR HOME.

Andrew (Husband & Best Friend). ♥

# August 10<sup>th</sup>

# NetFlixed!!

We are in the city of Barrie today (Barrie is a little more than an hour drive north of our Toronto home). We are here for a baseball tournament with Jabari and his team. Between innings and games, I am reflecting on the events of yesterday: a doctor's appointment, visit from family, and avoiding a near disastrous Netflix incident.

### The Family Doctor Checkup

Another successful six-week follow-up for Janise. Results of CT scans, blood, and other tests came back with good results. Janise is on point and remains free of pharmaceutical assistance.

Our carb free six out of seven- day meal plan is doing its "thang" and actually giving both of us good all-around medical improvements.

### The Visit From Family

We were pleasantly surprised by a visit from Janise's sister, Charmaine, and their mother, Eugenie. August 9th is Eugenie's birthday! The time spent was a blessing.

### The Netflix

Afterward, Janise and I decided to watch a mindless comedy on Netflix. To ensure there would be zero brain activity required we picked a Tyler Perry production starring Tiffany Haddish called *Nobody's Fool*.

Fun Fact: I am planning to ask God to add on 1 hour and 50 minutes to the lives of Janise and I; this being the full duration of the movie ***Nobody's Fool.*** Time we are hoping that God will replenish.

### The Netflix Incident

Unbeknownst to me, Janise was playing with my phone while we watched the surely "Academy Award" winning performances in this movie.

Not only did she tape 16 seconds of our conversation, she also sent this short audio out to approximately 200 people on my broadcast list in WhatsApp.

I became aware of this when I started to receive messages from my contacts regarding the recording they received!

To quote a childhood hero Elmer Fudd "Oh, the horrwah!"

After realizing the audio was permanent, I listen to it...it was mainly blank with the movie in the background and some inaudible commentary of mine about the movie.

In a word: phew!

I blame you Tyler Perry and Tiffany Haddish!

Fun Fact: Due to this additional stress, I am planning to ask God for five additional hours to the lives of Janise and I.

...from The City of Barrie.

Andrew (Husband & Best Friend). ♥

# August 16<sup>th</sup>

## Peace

### Time

Self-employment has provided us the freedom to enjoy each other's company each day at the office, the freedom to attend all medical and therapy appointments together, the freedom to spend our most precious commodity (time) based on our priorities.

Some may see our plate as being full, I say that our plate is actually fulfilling. We are the masters of our time. We get to spend this precious limited currency wisely on what we decide will provide us with the maximum tangible and intangible benefit.

### The Schedule

We have developed a manageable routine. On top of work and various medical and therapy appointments, we carefully fit in cooking get togethers, lunch, and visits with friends and family, as well as neighbourhood walks and exercise.

### Outpatient

Thankfully, Janise remains an outpatient of Providence Healthcare Centre and is able to continue receiving speech, physio, and occupational therapy.

Fun Fact: Janise is an inpatient at our home affording me the opportunity to offer some other types of...let's call it "Non-Medical" therapy that I cannot discuss at this or any other time .... LOL!

### Progress

Janise is moving literally. Moving physically with little supervision and assistance, moving mentally in terms of her memories with the assistance of journals and memory tasks, moving spiritually with her positive attitude towards recovery.

Playlist
## Peace in the Valley of Love by The Persuaders

...from OUR HOME.

Andrew (Husband & Best Friend). 💜

# August 24<sup>th</sup>

## Namaste

Namaste:

"I bow to the divine in you".

A greeting used in yoga, it is said with a slight bow, hands pressed together at the heart centre, palms touching, fingers pointing upwards, and thumbs close to the chest.

Cycling this hand position to the head, heart and mouth as a reminder to have clear and loving thoughts, intentions and communication.

We have incorporated yoga into our exercise routine. Yoga has played a key role in Janise regaining her overall balance. .

Mountain, tree, downward dog, upward dog, triangle, warrior 1, warrior 2, bridge, forward fold, and various twisting poses have many physical, mental and spiritual benefits.

Fun Fact: There is a certain visual benefit to downward dog...just sayin'.

### We All Need Some STIMULATION

We met with Janise's neurologist this week. Her most recent MRI indicated improvement to the stroke impacted areas of her brain. We receive reinforcement to continue to exercise Janise's brain.

Like other areas of the human body the brain has the capacity to grow. In the case of the brain, it is mental stimulation that improves and grows the brain function.

### THE WORK

So we continue THE WORK. Journals, talking, exercise, healthy eating, writing, reading, and mind games.

Namaste!

...from OUR HOME.

Andrew (Husband & Best Friend)

# August 29<sup>th</sup>

## Life

Life is "the condition that distinguishes animals and plants from inorganic matter, including the capacity for growth, reproduction, functional activity, and continual change preceding death."

We each experience life through our own eyes, our own perspective. Our lives narrated NOT by Morgan Freeman, but by that voice inside our head. Leading me to wonder, what is reality?

Real activities, events, words, and actions are subjected to this imperfect imprecise machine in our heads spitting out our own perspective.

We have the ability to make, shape, change, and ignore reality which is awesome, inspirational, crazy, and dangerous at the same damn time!.

Yes!/Yikes!

One thing that is REAL, changing your perspective can change your LIFE.

### The Social Butterfly

Fun Fake News: The name Janise is derived from the Latin word "occupatus" which means busy, busied, occupied, engaged, taken, employed.

I am officially Janise's Social Event Coordinator; keeping Mrs. Smith's event calendar on "The Google". Trust me she is soo "occupatus".

Coordinating lunches, dinners, BBQs, and other such gatherings, and visits at our home from friends and family. All arranged through "The Google" aka Google Calendar.

Fun Fact: The position of Janise's Social Event Coordinator is a paid position, but money is not the currency of choice, if ya know what I'm sayin'.

Damn! Need to get back to my social event coordinating, —the Obama's are calling again!

"No Michelle, I told you Janise has a hair appointment at 11:30am....Okay, Okay! When are you back in town?"

...from OUR HOME.

Andrew (Husband & Best Friend). 🖤

# September 1st

## That's LOVE

*On the BIG Ferris Wheel at the Canadian National Exhibition (CNE, aka The EX)*

Playlist
**That's LOVE by Oddisee**

...from The CNE.

Andrew (Husband & Best Friend). 🖤

# September 15<sup>th</sup>

## "Open"

It has been six months!

On March 18, 2019, our lives changed. We did not simply slowdown from our current path, we STOPPED.

Everything halted. No motion. Even breathing became difficult and laboured as the air surrounding us was cloudy and heavy. Life, laughter, and LOVE replaced by illness, sadness, & and tears.

The LOVE remained though, it was now accompanied by its new partners: hopes and prayers.

OPEN

We remained OPEN!

OPEN to beating the odds of a stroke to both the left and right side of Janise's thalamas. The thalamas is what the doctors describe as the "brain within the brain - the mini brain", responsible for:

- directing signals throughout the brain (it is the brains traffic cop)
- some motor movement, including eyes & one close to my heart; swallowing
- memories
- consciousness & unconsciousness

Through Janise's hard work in recovery, we are encouraged by her progress.

Keeping us:

- OPEN to her potential; and
- OPEN to the possibilities.

Our path no longer halted, we are once again in motion. In motion on a new rugged path which is currently under construction.

This new path is not a smooth one, yet it remains beautiful. It's potholes and sink holes forcing us to zig, zag and leap on the way.

However, on this new path we are enjoying the journey and are less concerned about the destination.

Playlist
## Open by Da Beatminerz
## (featuring Caron Wheeler & Pete Rock)

...from OUR HOME.

Andrew (Husband & Best Friend). 🖤

# September 20<sup>th</sup>

## On the Move

Janise is on the MOVE!

Now confidently moving up and down the stairs in our home. Scaring me at first by sneaking off behind my back to gain her independence.

It has been difficult for me as my instinct is to hover around her to prevent a potential slip or fall. My overprotective behaviour is often met with:

- "I am OK!";
- "Go ahead of me"; and
- "Leave me alone!".

Understandably over the last six months, this once independent, high performing, multitasking entrepreneur and event planner has been:

- Hospitalized;
- Poked;
- Prodded; and
- Monitored.

She now fights for her independence.

Janise is no longer institutionalized, and we are cutting back on the monitoring.

Fun Fact: My intention is NEVER EVER to cut back on the POKING & PRODDING LOL!

This week we attended the Annual General Meeting of The Jamaican Canadian Association of Nurses (JCAN).

Janise is on the MOVE!

Janise continues to be a member of the Board of this AMAZING organization. JCAN has been a GREAT supporter and cheerleader for Janise during her illness.

Thank you JCAN for the LOVE, support and respect you continued to show to my QUEEN. Your actions speak volumes to the values on which JCAN was founded.

Evidence of the temporary nature of Janise's illness continues to be revealed. The storm has passed, the clouds remain, yet the promise of the new sun is in the forecast.

Playlist
## Just a Cloud Away by Pharrell Williams

...from OUR HOME.

Andrew (Husband & Best Friend) 🖤

# September 21<sup>st</sup>

## "I WILL"

Reflections

**July 25, 1992**

Reverend Patrick Reid of www.thecornerstone.ca asked a question that is still fresh in my mind.

"...to have and to hold, from this day forward, for better, for worse, for richer, for poorer, in sickness and in health, to love and to cherish, till death do us part, according to God's holy ordinance?"

I looked into the eyes of my beautiful bride while the onlookers, Janise's parents, my parents, family and friends in the packed church looked on in quiet anticipation on that steaming hot summer day.

The answer to Reverend Reid's question rolled off of my tongue with the arrogant, loud, and pride filled confidence of a young man overflowing with testosterone (Note: all of this testosterone being produced naturally).

I responded in a LOUD CONFIDENT voice that overwhelmed the silence within the church - "I WILL!!"

**December 4, 2000**

I went under the knife. Four hours of surgery to remove a brain tumor located on my pituitary gland (A BIG shout out to Dr. Cusimano of St. Mike's hospital).

During this time Janise reminded me of Reverend Reid's question and repeated her answer - "I WILL!!"

**March 18, 2019**

Janise suffers a massive stroke. During this time I remind Janise of Reverend Reid's question and repeated my answer

- "I WILL!!"

Playlist
## I Will by Prince

...from OUR HOME.

Andrew (Husband & Best Friend) 🖤

# September 23$^{rd}$

## Tour Guide

Janise was a temporary resident of The Scarborough General Hospital from mid- March to late April, and subsequently a resident of Providence Healthcare Centre (the rehabilitation hospital) from late April until the end of May.

**Providence Healthcare Centre**

Janise has speech, physio and occupational therapy at Providence weekly. Hence, I have been able to take her to her former room at Providence. Show her our old walking routines, our food spot (Tim Hortons restaurant in Providence), the chapel, and our makeout spots.

The best part of the tour is meeting up with the nurse staff to show them the results of their work through Janise's successes; they truly do God's work.

**Scarborough General Hospital**

Today, after Janise's appointment at Scarborough General Hospital, I get back into tour guide mode. I show Janise where she stayed in ICU and the hospital ward. The ICU is a double-edged sword, bring back many painful memories of breathing tubes, feeding tubes, and various medical monitoring devices; but also professional, positive, encouraging, and empathetic nurses, cleaning staff, technicians, and doctors working towards the goal of preserving LIFE.

This walk down memory lane did stimulate Janise's memories. She was very familiar with the room she stayed in at ICU;, her hospital ward room was less familiar to her.

The staff was happy to see Janise and thanked us for coming by to see them.

Words fail to express our gratitude towards both of these hospitals.

We show our gratitude in how we continue to LOVE, LAUGH, SMILE, and SHINE each day of our lives.

Playlist
## Stay High by Brittany Howard

...from OUR HOME.

Andrew (Husband & Best Friend) ♥

# September 27<sup>th</sup>

## "Who Are You"

### Who U R

You are the culmination of your thoughts and actions. Not just that which you carefully handcraft and present to the world, but also the thoughts and actions that are hidden and protected by you.

These latter thoughts and actions can be very personal and at times inconsistent with the picture that you have painted for us to view.

### Who We R

These last seven months have been a reintroduction to my wife. Yes, I have known Janise from Sir Ernest MacMillan Senior Public School (Grade 8 to be exact) but I continue to be amazed at who she is, and who I am with Janise.

In sickness, Janise was at the lowest point that I have seen her in my life. My mission became that of an advocate, ensuring that all actions taken on her behalf were to her ultimate benefit and maintained her dignity; a tremendously overwhelming responsibility.

Today Janise's memory is still in repair, however, she continues to maintain her core character.

Janise's character is consistent whether viewed in the outside world or behind closed doors. This is what first attracted me to her aura and continues to keep me addicted to her LOVE:

- Strength;
- Intelligence;
- Resilience;
- Patience;
- Humour;
- Determination;
- Beauty; and
- Unconditional LOVE.

So much of who I am has come from Janise, and who I am with Janise.

I am evolving into the best of who we are together and continue to learn about Janise, myself and who we are.

**Who R U?**

Playlist
## Who Are You by Bilal

...from OUR HOME.

Andrew (Husband & Best Friend) 🖤

# September 29<sup>th</sup>

## The Seeds

To the young men Janise and I created:

(for the purpose of time I will leave the details of this creation process for another day.....you're welcome).

Jabari and Jelani I say: Time is REAL!

The earth continues to circle the sun in constant measurement of our time, and we have no control over it's passage.

We do however control what we do within its boundaries. Make GOOD decisions, make your time COUNT and mean something at least to ONE person outside of U.

U then will truly see the rewards that life has to offer.

...With ♥ from DAD

# October 8<sup>th</sup>

## What is it All About?

Playlist
**It's not about... By Lloyd Brown**

The pace of life has changed, it has slowed down significantly from the previous continuous sprint. However slower our movements the purpose of our movements have never been more clear.

Gone are the tasks that lead to nowhere, those tasks that fill our day and provide zero benefit. They have specifically been replaced with new tasks that meet our goals and intentions.

**On This Day: We Play Hooky from Work.**

The day was bright and warm, the sun high in the sky; literally calling out to us to take advantage of this warm Autumn day. It took very little convincing; we do live in the north where the brisk, heartless cold of winter is our inevitable reality.

We take a long walk down in The Guild (a beautiful neighbourhood in Scarborough, near Lake Ontario). Our travels taking us past various schools with a stop off at a coffee shop, and at Janise's hair salon for a redo of her twist hair style.

On This Day: We break from our normal routine and rediscover our neighbourhood and each other .

This Is What It's All About .

...from OUR HOME.

Andrew (Husband & Best Friend). 💜

# October 11<sup>th</sup>

## Happy Birthday

This one is extra special, as we were reminded this year to take nothing for granted. Life is precious and fragile, a fact that is often forgotten as we navigate our busy lives.

Your birthday ironically kicks off Thanksgiving weekend in Canada, and our family is once again reminded of the blessings we have received in just this year.

We are blessed to watch our son Jabari play the last baseball tournament of 2019 with his team in Canton, Ohio this weekend!

We get inspiration from watching both of our children (Jelani and Jabari) set and accomplish their goals. They provide us with that much needed youthful and carefree energy to refuel.

On the day of your birth, I remind you that you have come far and that it has been a long road. I urge you to continue...

Continue 2 FIGHT!

Continue 2 THRIVE!

Continue 2 LOVE!

Continue 2 BE!

Playlist
**The Lion of Judah (Conquering Lion) by Bob Marley and The Wailers**

...from Canton, Ohio us

Andrew (Husband & Best Friend). 🖤

# October 29<sup>th</sup>

## Where is President Obama?

Memories are mostly rooted in real events that are subject to the inherent imperfections of each of our individual interpretations.

When we are all in agreement about a particular "memorable" event, our recall of the details of this event will never produce an exact match; this is our collective memories running at top form; at best!

Sadly, with the passage of time a memory can fade, change, or simply disappear. But that same memory can be rediscovered once again in the present day as:

- your senses pick up a particular aroma;

- you hear a familiar song;

- someone says a phrase that you-know-you-know!; and

- you experience a deja vu moment, triggered by a visit to a particular place.

**The Short & Long**

Janise's short-term memory is showing signs of recovery. The journaling of our daily activities, rehab, and memory tasks have been helpful.

Her long-term memory is a puzzle.

There are gaps in time.

Not remembering the passing of certain family members, then realizing it through conversation or a random memory opens up fresh wounds.

In these moment...everything STOPS! RAW emotions pour out...sadness and anger!

Then...the memory goes away just as quickly as it came. However, this scenario will reoccur randomly in the near future.

The future scenarios however are now more and more the result of Janise's memory recall. This shows the good sign that these memories are becoming more and more accessible to her.

There is one memory that Janise is not able to reconcile, and it comes up every time we watch the news.

Janise asks the oh soo familiar question:

"Where is President Barack Obama? I thought that he was the president of America."

Now it was my turn

In this moment...everything STOPS!

RAW emotions pour out...sadness and anger!

LOL!


...from OUR HOME.


Andrew (Husband & Best Friend). 💜

# November 8<sup>th</sup>

## Moments

A moment is a period of time.

It is not something that can be measured with precision, there is no official scale that measures a moment. As such a moment can be as short as an instant or can last for an extended period of time.

Moments are a series of events, a feeling, a special occasion.

Moments are:

- Good, bad, ugly, and sad;

- Special, awesome, spiritual, and tragic.

The joining of each of our individual moments tell the story of our lives.

**How We Livin'**

Janise's memory issues emphasize the importance of each moment in our lives.

Emotions, thoughts, and feelings can be fluid. They have the potential to change radically from moment to moment based on how the mind is being stimulated. The mind constantly works through an influx of information; and is able to parse through and make sense of information by using current and past knowledge and memories.

Knowledge and memories are the strong foundation on which our sense of self is based. When this foundation is disrupted our moments can also be disrupted.

The BEAUTY is we are built to learn, we never lose our propensity to learn. So that's what we'll do; LEARN! and RELEARN!

This week we attended a support group at Providence Healthcare Centre - Living With Stroke. This group has been the source of excellent stroke information, strategies for prevention and life after stroke.

Mostly though this group is yet another reminder that we are not alone in this battle, this battle is not for the swift but for those who can endure, and that the battle can be WON! If we remain ONE!

...from OUR HOME.

Andrew (Husband & Best Friend).

# November 9<sup>th</sup>

## "Alright"

### The Fight

In my youth, it was in the form of fighting against something. Societal structure, norms, and wrongs.

Now the fight continues, but it has changed slightly. My focus is to fight for something or someone.

The protagonists: my now expanded family.

The antagonist has also expanded to now include health along with the ever present and unrelenting societal ills.

### The Work

It's HARD!

There is a recognition that the number of things we control is generally overshadowed by the things we do not control. Yet there are things we do control!

Focusing on the things we do control can and will impact our situation for the better.

Reflecting and reminiscing on the past emphasizing the shoulda, coulda, wounda scenarios is a waste of time. Past performance as a benchmark for future improvement is a much better utilization of the past.

So, I fight for the protagonist Janise in this real life situation. I use the past benchmark of Janise pre-stroke with the realization of how far we have come from that day when our world STOPPED - March 18, 2019.

We have since, and continue to be, ON-THE-MOVE and deep in the fight.

- Dukes up!

- Roll with the punches!

- Counter punch!

- Get ON-THE-ATTACK!

I am handling this situation well as a result of the culmination of my life experiences; I know and believe that we 'gon be alright!

Playlist
## Alright by Kendrick Lamar

...from OUR HOME.

Andrew (Husband & Best Friend). 🖤

# November 15<sup>th</sup>

## The Same Boat

We R ALL in The Same Boat

Merilyn is an energetic Jamaican born grandmother who stands around five feet tall, sports a beautiful round grey short afro and is dressed in comfortable sportswear.

She is a proud, strong Christian woman who walks with the assistance of a walker; the walker being the only visible impact of the wounds inflicted by the stroke that she experienced in the summer of 2019.

On this day of the meeting of the Life After Stroke Group at Providence Healthcare she opens up about her life and experiences, pre-stroke, during her stroke and after her stroke.

The group is comprised of stroke survivors, family caregivers, and two group leaders/ moderators (Vanessa and Mary) who work at Providence and have been running these groups for almost a decade.

There are approximately 20 of us listening intently to Merilyn, you could hear a pin drop. We learn about a hardworking, independent, loving, stubborn, family focused woman. This small glimpse into her world provide us with a roller coaster of emotions, it is a ride we are all willing to take with her.

There are tears, tissues, laughter, and important lessons. We learn from her experiences and receive reinforcement that although our life journeys may differ, we are all in the same boat now.

What is most relatable is Merilyn's adjustment from independence to dependence and the fight to get back to independence. Merilyn is living our experience as we are living Merilyn's.

### Blood Clot/Blood Claat

*(2-mat-toe/2-mate-toe)*

I did feel the need to call Merilyn out though. In the description of her stroke, she continued to use foul language, talking of certain unmentionables blocking vessels in her brain.

Like Merilyn, Janise and I are of Jamaican heritage. Janise was born in Trelawny, Jamaica, I was born in Bristol, England of Jamaican parents.

The word "Blood Claat" is a curse word in Jamaica. Merilyn continued the use of this term in the explanation of her stroke. I had simply had enough of her vulgar, profane speech and finally felt the need to correct Merilyn:

"Merilyn, I understand that you have experienced a great trauma but there is NO excuse for your language! Please stop the swearing! I mean the term Blood Claat. Really!" Laughter erupted in the room LOL!

...from OUR HOME.

Andrew (Husband & Best Friend). ♥

# November 27ᵗʰ

## LOVE & FEAR

Coming up to the end of November 2019, we have passed the eight-month mark since Janise experienced a stroke.

We all live within the constraints of TIME.

TIME, that double edge sword, the ultimate giver and taker of all things within this life.

Understanding this reality assists with the acceptance of whatever human condition we are currently confronted with at any given TIME.

With TIME we have :

· Gained knowledge, perspective, patience, and HOPE (LOVE); and

· Lost indecisiveness, shame, and FEAR.

The ultimate battle that we all face at each moment of TIME: LOVE v.s. FEAR.

Let's get ready to RUMBLE!

Playlist
### Love by Erykah Badu

**LOVE**

We have completed all of the outpatient therapy sessions at Providence Healthcare Centre and have brought all that we have learned back HOME, to Scarborough!

We continue the connection to Providence through various day programs, and the medical community through various visits, consultation and tests.

**FEAR?**

Got NONE!

...from OUR HOME.

Andrew (Husband & Best Friend).

# The Miracle

We're now ready to confront:
- the GOOD;
- the BAD; and
- the UGLY.

### The Good

Janise is physically and mentally doing a majority of the things she was able to do pre-stroke. I will leave out the non-PG details.

### The Bad

Janise struggles with short-term memory recall, her long-term memory is at times non-linear, she suffers random balancing issues, and her vision has been impacted (unable to move her eyes vertically and focus on text consistently).

### The Ugly

I fill in any gaps in Janise's memory with "alternative facts" that are advantageous to ME! (insert evil maniacal laugh here!).

### The Miracle

In our appointment with Janise's neurologist this week at Scarborough General Hospital he expressed his amazement at Janise's progress so far.

He spoke in non-medical terms; sharing our faith, optimism, and excitement on Janise's potential as evidenced by how far Janise has recovered to date:
* From coma;
* To bedridden;
* To wheelchair;
* To walking; to
* More and more!
To be continued....

...from OUR HOME.

Andrew (Husband & Best Friend). ♥

# December 19<sup>th</sup>

## "I'll Rise"

Life can at times feel like a tragic play with a series of events leading to a predictable and unfavourable conclusion.

We are more TIMEs than not left with questions and emptiness as we search for the purpose and meaning behind the events of our lives.

TIME provides us with snippets of information allowing reflection, giving us the ability to gain perspective, and most important the space to heal.

TIME can give us the gift of meaning, but not always. Some TIMEs the events of our lives simply highlight our vulnerabilities and reveal to us and the world the inner strength we never knew that we possessed.

Janise is improving each day, although many of our questions about the future and outcomes remain unanswered, we have moved on.

**Moved on from:**

· Questioning; and

· Emptiness.

**Moved on to:**

· Purpose; and

· Healing.

**The Secret?**

It's not a secret at all, it is simply TIME. As TIME allows, we continue to RISE!

Playlist
**I'll Rise by Ben Harper (Poem by Maya Angelou)**

...from OUR HOME.

Andrew (Husband & Best Friend).

# March 18<sup>th</sup>

## 2020 – One Year In

This day is truly a lifetime away from March 18, 2019. A year ago,

Our family had just returned home from St. Petersburg, Florida. Life as we knew it would change. Stroke, Coma, and the beginning of a 2 1/2 month hospital stay.

From HOME to Scarborough General Hospital to Providence Health Care and back HOME. Travelling through ICU to the hospital ward to rehabilitation to outpatient care within the Canadian health care universe.

And today 3-18-20:

We are thankful for Janise's progress and recognize that we are not done with the recovery journey. Our new normal prioritizes mental, physical, and spiritual health. Mental and physical exercises, supplements, nutrition, and the careful management of our most precious commodity; time.

The Future?:

We approach our future with an excitement and openness particularly at this time of madness and mass hysteria created by COVID-19:

- #toiletpaperLOVE
- #3plyisMYply
- #1plyisCRAP
- #NOpaper
- #washYOURbutt

In this journey our family has seen the unexpected and unlikely outcome of an event where the "experts" had painted a grim and tragic picture.

We have now taken control of our canvas. We have no idea what the final painting will look like, but we choose to fill our canvas with bright and bold colours filled with LOVE.

...from OUR HOME.

Andrew (Husband & Best Friend). 🖤

# AFTERWORDS

**STROKE**

This small six letter word has changed our lives. Initially impacting our lives negatively; now we simply make lemonade with the lemons we have been served. Previously I associated the word STROKE with joyous activities: back STROKE, side STROKE, front STROKE. I am of course referring to SWIMMING, one of my favourite activities (or am I?).

The messed-up thing about a STROKE is the very fact that you had a STROKE increases the probability of getting a STROKE!

How is that fair?

It seems like some kind of evil sadistic loop.

There are many things within OUR control that WE can do to reduce the probability of STROKE and NOT repeat the ride within this evil sadistic loop.

**1. Nutrition**

Read the labels of all the foods you eat! Watch what YOU put in your mouth (...by now you know what I'm thinking. This kind of comedy just writes itself)! Avoid the legal drugs of sodium, sugar, and trans fats.

**2. Supplements**

Food ain't what it used to be. We actually need to take supplements to get the vitamins we need. Do your research! We are on:

- Vitamins B,C,D
- Magnesium
- Co-Q10, Fish Oil
- Natto kinase
- Probiotics
- Glucosamine

### 3. Exercise

We exercise daily. Exercise for mental, physical, and spiritual health. For your loved ones so YOU live longer. For YOU so YOU live without pain. Endure the pain of exercise now so YOU do not feel the pain that comes with age.

We continue to work on Janise's memory. Depending on when you catch her, we can be anywhere on the spectrum of our life together. Boyfriend and girlfriend, engaged, newlyweds or married.

Fun Fact: At any point in time my woman can be a hot young girlfriend, an energetic newlywed, or an experienced older woman. God is Good, ALL THE TIME!

We are strangers, continuing to learn about who we have become since Janise's stroke. Now creating a new normal; new memories, accomplishments, wins, losses, habits, and mannerisms.

Many things do however remain the same. Janise's disgust at the way I eat. Apparently like a pig? Must be the grunting. Her irritation at my OCD when it comes to, well, EVERYTHING, and her great LOVE and support of all that is Andrew.

We are familiar strangers on a continuous journey of discovery.

Actually rediscovery.

Everyday offers more evidence that we are one: where I end Janise begins, where Janise ends I begin. I am truly defined through Janise as she is with me.

Playlist
# Nothing Without You by Tanerélle

### Ground Hog Day

"Where is Jelani?"

"Where is Jabari?"

"What day is it today?"

"What are we doing today?"

The day has begun, the same way it started yesterday. Janise first inquiring about her beloved pickney, then trying to get hold of her own reality in time and space.

I go through the ritual of uploading Janise's mainframe with data to catch her up from the period where her mind has been stalled. The length and information in this upload vary from day to day but its existence is a constant.

My role begins:

"Jelani has his own place, yes he is 25 years old and a university graduate. He works as a Real Estate Agent."

"Jabari is in his room soon to jump on an online class; his high school is physically closed due to the COVID-19 virus."

Recognizing the sadness in her eyes, I then detail why she does not know information that every mother should know about her children, "Hun, you had a stroke".

At times Janise accepts my word, other times proof must be provided. Hospital documents, pictures, the video I made explaining everything (which Janise appears in and plays leading role).

Now uplifted and convinced (hew!):

- I cook breakfast.

- We eat.

- We take our supplements.

- We exercise (yoga, weights, or kickboxing).

- We shower.

- Get dressed.

We are then ready to conquer the day!

The day ends usually with us crashed on the living room couch, with the TV closely watching us, and us struggling up to our bedroom.

Hours from now this process will restart from the beginning.

Gladly, I look forward to the challenges of the morning with Janise Smith as I am thankful that She is HERE with ME.

#SheisHereWithMe


...from OUR HOME.


Andrew (Husband & Best Friend). ❤

# ACKNOWLEDGEMENTS

I would like to thank all of the people who have supported our family during this trying time in our lives. Know that you are and remain to be the fuel that we need most, to make it through our days.

The strength that I gained from your support enabled me to put together the contents of this book to share with you and the rest of the world. It is my wish that the pages in this book will help guide and support others, as our family has been.

I pass on your love and support through these humble notes.

It would be an impossible task to list the many involved in creating this work. Its existence is the culmination of the support our family received and continues to receive throughout this stroke journey. This support provides the fuel needed to make it through each day; it arrives right on time. Never too early and never too late. Never too quick and never too slow.

My thanks go out to all who have supported our family—period.

All of you provided me the strength to put together the contents of this book, this book that I now share with you and the rest of the world.

This book would not be possible without my friend, Julie Thompson, who introduced me to this world of writing—thank you! Then my amazing editor, Akosua Jackie Brown, and her team took over to turn the words into a book—thank you all, too!

It is my wish that the pages of this book will help guide and support others as our family has been supported. Through these humble notes, I pass on the love and support I have received to you, the reader.

To the reader: tag—you're "it"!

Spread the love 🖤 ☺

Andrew

# ABOUT THE AUTHOR

Andrew Smith is a son, brother, nephew, cousin, uncle, husband, and father. He is also an accounting professional (a certified professional accountant and a chartered accountant) and now a published author.

With his high energy, rambunctious personality, and love of family, Andrew is known for having a unique ("special") sense of humour and a hearty, evil, loud, villain-type laugh. It is best not to be on the receiving end of his disturbing laughter.

As demonstrated in this book, Andrew's deep love of music is wide ranged. He loves anything from ska, rock steady, reggae, rock and roll, punk, funk, house, disco, jazz, calypso, hip hop, and rhythm and blues to the music from the African continent. He also has a passion for cooking, baking, exercise, overall health, and writing!

Andrew has been fortunate to share the majority of his lifetime with his wife and best friend, Janise Smith, the subject of this book. It is through the love of this beautiful woman, that this book has been conceived, birthed, documented, and now shared. It is the hope of this author that your reading experience will be as healing to you as was his experience writing the contents.

# Lost and found: by my side

You are here with me, by my side.

I feel your warmth.

Your love, your smile and your touch.
In you I continue to see that which is familiar.

I feel a sense of comfort and joy as I watch you navigate your
new world and your new mind, in your new body.

Yet these things  you find new are not new to you at all. They
are merely a rediscovery of you from the past.

Your facial expression when you are joyous, angry, confused
and sad. The way you stroll, dance and move.

Your dimples, that giggle, and gut belly laugh. The joy you
bring to all within your orbit.

You are there!

You are here with me, by my side.

Lost and found; by my side.